LEADING SCHOOLS IN T

HEADS OF DEPARTMENT

ESSAYS IN LEADERSHIP
FOR CHANGING TIMES

Edited by

Brenda Despontin and Nigel Richardson

Published for the Girls' Schools Association and
the Headmasters' and Headmistresses' Conference
by John Catt Educational Ltd
2008

First Published 2008

by John Catt Educational Ltd,
12 Deben Mill Business Centre, Old Maltings Approach,
Melton, Woodbridge, Suffolk IP12 1BL
Tel: 01394 389850 Fax: 01394 386893
Email: enquiries@johncatt.co.uk
Website: www.johncatt.com

ISBN: 978 1 904724 65 0

Set and designed by
John Catt Educational Limited

Printed and bound in Great Britain
by Bell & Bain, Glasgow, Scotland

CONTENTS

About the Contributors

Jill Berry became Head of Dame Alice Harpur School in Bedford in 2000, following five years as deputy head at Nottingham High School for Girls GDST. She was educated at a co-ed grammar school, which became a comprehensive during her time there, in South Yorkshire during the 1970s. She holds an honours degree in English from Manchester University and went on to obtain a PGCE and later a masters' degree from Liverpool. She has taught in a variety of schools, maintained and independent, comprehensive and selective, all girls, all boys and co-ed, since 1980. Jill was a member of the GSA inspections committee from 2004 and served as chairman of the committee in 2007. She is currently president-elect of the Girls' Schools Association and will become president from January 2009.

Dr Michael Carslaw is Headmaster of St Leonards School in Fife. Previously he was deputy head of Ardingly College in West Sussex and head of science of the City of London Freemen's School. He has experience of working in a range of independent schools, both boarding and day. His interest in the teacher culture of independent schools, and how it is related to effective professional development and performance management, stems from his time spent completing a PhD at the Institute of Education, University of London, and an MBA at the University of Nottingham. He was awarded the BELMAS prize for the best PhD thesis in 2006 and has enjoyed discussing his interests in this field as course director of the annual IPD CPD co-ordinators' conference and elsewhere.

Margot Chaundler OBE was bursar of St Paul's Girls' School for 13 years, having been one of the first women appointed to the administrative class of the Ministry of Defence. She served as governor of the Haberdashers' Aske's Schools at Elstree for 11 years, and for nine years as vice-chairman and governor of an inner London Church of England primary school. She is currently a member of council of Roedean School, and has recently become a governor of a new Haberdashers' Company Academy.

Dr Brenda Despontin became principal of the British School in Brussels in September 2008, and was previously Headmistress of Haberdashers' Monmouth School for Girls since 1997. She has a first degree in psychology, a master's degree in Thomas Hardy, a doctorate in children's literature and an MBA on educational leadership. After teaching at the British School in Brussels and working as a residential supervisor in a home for disturbed teenage girls, she went on to teach at comprehensive and independent schools before setting up the girls' division at the King's School in Macclesfield. She was president of GSA in 2006.

Edward Elliott has been Head of the Perse School in Cambridge since September 2008, where he taught geography and politics for the previous 11 years – a period during which he was also successively head of the sixth form, director of studies and senior deputy head. He graduated from St Anne's College, Oxford, and worked in industry before starting his teaching career at Whitgift School.

Nick Fisher became head of physics at Rugby in 1994 and he has been head of science there since 1998. He currently teaches physics and astronomy and has also taught drama. Since 2003 he has been the independent state school partnership co-ordinator for Rugby, a role which aims to promote science throughout local schools. He has been a Nuffield A level examiner, an ISI inspector and was involved in the piloting of Salters Horners advanced physics. In 2003 he was Salters physics teacher of the year and in 2005 was elected a Fellow of the Institute of Physics. In 2007 he led the physics team which pioneered the new Cambridge Pre-U physics course. His main interests are drama and the history of science and he has developed a number of public understanding of science lectures incorporating these themes.

Jane Gandee studied Spanish and French at Cambridge University, and moved into teaching via accountancy. Her first jobs were at Lord Wandsworth College in Hampshire and at Oakham School. She spent two years as head of Spanish and six years as head of languages at Queenswood School in Hertfordshire before moving to City of London School for Girls, where she is currently director of studies.

Andrew Grant has been Headmaster of St Albans School since 1993. In previous existences he was second master at the Royal Grammar School, Guildford; head of English and drama at Whitgift School, Croydon; and taught English at Merchant Taylors' School, Northwood. He has been involved in drama, and also in sport of various kinds, throughout his teaching career. He was co-chair of the HMC/GSA education/academic policy committee from 2002-2005 and sat on various other curriculum-related groups including the assessment sub-group of the Tomlinson 14-19 Review and the HMC/GSA universities sub-committee. A governor of a number of prep schools and of a GSA school, he was chairman of HMC London division 2006-2007 and has been elected HMC chairman for 2009-2010.

Frances Green has a MSc Econ (Information Management) from University of Wales, Aberystwyth, and has spent over 25 years working in education. In addition to overseeing a lively and well-used library resource centre at Haberdashers' Monmouth School for Girls she has held a number of posts including head of general studies, key skills co-ordinator and currently is gifted and talented co-ordinator. The assessment of learning styles at HMSG has developed into an ongoing programme throughout the school during the past eight years and she has organised and run INSET sessions on the topic both in-house and externally. In addition she has been a governor, and chair of governors of a local primary school and as a freelance writer has contributed articles to national newspapers and magazines on education and the family and also on historical topics.

Melanie Lincoln has been head of economics and business studies at Dame Alice Harpur School since 2002. She is also senior tutor to the sixth form. She holds an honours degree in commerce and French from Birmingham University, a PGCE in economics and business studies from Manchester University, and took an MA in educational leadership at Nottingham University. She previously taught at Bedford School for three years, where she was an assistant boarding housemistress, and a second lieutenant and security officer in the CCF. She has been responsible for Young Enterprise in both schools, and has contributed to *Economics Today* for their Back to Basics column.

Kathryn Macaulay is Director of ICT and Data systems at The Abbey School, Reading. She has worked for 17 years in GSA schools teaching, managing and leading design and technology and ICT (academic and MIS). She is an ISI inspector, a member of the ISC ICT experts group and an Adobe Education Leader presenting and consulting nationally and globally in ICT Education.

Dr John Newton is Headmaster of Taunton School, before which he was director of studies and later housemaster at Eastbourne College. A graduate of Merton College, Oxford, with a degree in French and Russian, John also has a PhD in 'the organisational culture of independent schools'. John and his wife Catherine have four young children, who attend Taunton School.

Alice Phillips has been Head of St Catherine's, Bramley, a GSA school in Surrey, since 2000. She was deputy head at Tormead School, Guildford, from 1993-1999 and prior to that completed ten years as a member of the English department at the Royal Masonic School, Rickmansworth, with four years as head of department. She serves on the GSA/HMC professional development committee, is chairman of the GSA's south central region, and a governor of a specialist music school. A graduate of Kendal High School for Girls, and Newnham College, Cambridge, she has also been a member of the Newnham College Roll committee.

Dr Nigel Richardson was Head of the Perse School, Cambridge, from 1994 to 2008, having been second master at Uppingham, Head of the Dragon School, Oxford, and deputy head of the King's School in Macclesfield. He is a governor of several HMC schools, and was editor of the HMC magazine *Conference & Common Room* from 1999 to 2002. He has written history books for children and training literature for the Industrial Society, and contributes regularly to the educational press. He was chairman of HMC in 2007, and amongst other writing projects is currently working on a biography of the great Victorian Headmaster Edward Thring.

Shane Rutter-Jerome has been general secretary of AGBIS since 2003 and is himself a school governor. Prior to this he spent seven years as bursar and clerk at Cranleigh School. His first career was in the Army: from Sandhurst he joined the Royal Artillery, serving worldwide for 30 years but missing most wars. He studied and instructed at Army and Joint Service staff colleges and was a head of department at Camberley. His last appointment was Commandant, Royal School of Artillery. He has continued his contact with his regiment and chaired its officer selection board for five years.

Paul Todd was born in 1963 and attended a state grammar school in Rastrick in West Yorkshire. He was awarded a double-first in physics by Cambridge University, but after beginning his PhD he found teaching the undergraduates more rewarding than his research, and after a period of travel he moved into secondary education. He has taught at a wide variety of schools: Slindon College; Strathallan School; Tonbridge School; and Norwich School. At Tonbridge he was head of physics, head of science, and then a housemaster. He is now at Norwich School as principal deputy head.

Introduction

Nigel Richardson

This is the third volume in the series of *Leading Schools in the 21st Century*. The first, published in 2007, looked at issues affecting the day-to-day lives of Heads; the second (2008) dealt largely with matters involving members of senior management teams.

In volume three we focus on heads of department (HoDs). They have become crucially important middle managers in most secondary schools in recent years. Their roles and responsibilities have grown out of all recognition (as the opening section of this book will show). With increasing moves towards devolved budgets, a good working relationship with the bursar as well as the Head has become highly important: hence the fact that this collection includes a general description of the demands on a bursar, as well as a more specific one about the inter-action between bursar and HoD.

In volume four we plan to examine the pastoral demands on boarding house-parents, section heads in day schools and others with similar responsibilities; and in volume five to look at issues and expectations on NQTs and other entrants to the profession. It is hoped that both these publications will appear in 2009.

Meanwhile this marks the third and final volume co-sponsored by the Girls' Schools Association (GSA), and the last one co-edited by Brenda Despontin, who is now becoming an HMC international member as she takes up her post as Principal of the British School in Brussels. My sincere thanks to them both.

Chapter 1

HODs: an overview

Nigel Richardson

Leaving school for the last time makes you reflective. When I recently spent some time thinking about all the changes in personnel which schools have experienced since I began teaching in 1970, I came to the view that no single role had changed more dramatically than that of the head of department (HoD).

Head teachers deal with ever-increasing paperwork, legal complexities and social fall-out. Boarding school house-parents and their counterparts in day schools (including age-related section heads) have smaller teaching allocations than they once did; they cope with a huge variety of pastoral issues, engaging with a growing band of nursing and counselling agencies in the process. But for all these groups it is the *balance* of their roles which has changed rather than the essential nature of the roles themselves.

One level below the Head there has been a major evolution from long-standing senior figures such as second masters to younger deputies who are soon-to-be Heads (as explored in volume two of this series), but you could argue that the change here is as much in the type of person holding the job as in what that job entails. Working alongside them, directors of studies are a comparatively recent invention, emerging as they did a generation ago from the ranks of those who once merely 'did the timetable'.

Heads of department, on the other hand, have existed for many years; they have always been, and continue to be, responsible for the academic side of a school's life. And yet in the past few decades the role, scope and importance of the HoD have undergone a complete transformation. In the process, so has the status of the job – especially in boarding schools.

In the schools in which I worked in the first half of my career, it would be fair to say that it was in the housemasters' meetings that the real power lay – something which was a great source of frustration to many HoDs.

Nowadays the balance of that power is likely to be rather more evenly spread between the two, and there is a much greater mutual respect and valuing of the work of each of the two groups.

There is a risk, I am conscious, of undervaluing what HoDs did in earlier times, but apart from often teaching the top sets (including the highly stimulating, rewarding and very personal seventh-term Oxbridge teaching which was swept away in 1984), much of their role was essentially administrative: ordering the textbooks and seeing to the setting of pupils.

It was left to the Head and his or her immediate lieutenants to deal with personnel matters, and if HoDs spent much time considering possible new teaching styles or learning methods, they did not always talk about them. Departmental meetings might take place only rarely, and could hardly be described as being deeply embedded in the school's culture.

Change was far less rapid and continuous, too. Public exams changed comparatively little, either in fundamental form or detailed syllabus. Unless my memory plays tricks, the history O level syllabus which I taught from 1971 to 1986 remained almost exactly the same, except that *England: 1914-64* became *England: 1914-74* – and even that small change was made in two stages. At A level over the period 1971-89 the two outlines papers remained virtually unaltered; only the special subject changed, in a way that was hardly dramatic – from four questions to three – and the topics studied for that paper remained on the syllabus for six to eight years.

By contrast, over the past 20 years we have had the introduction of the National Curriculum, of GCSE, IGCSE, Curriculum 2000, and the IB. There are further changes to both A level and GCSE still to come, the arrival of the Pre-U exam, the Diploma and so on. Modular arrangements, coursework (in both the BI and AI eras: before and after the internet), and the introduction of AS levels have added further dimensions and complexities.

In the same period there have been fundamental changes in respect of the HoD's role towards departmental staff. Retention of good teachers has become a major issue – especially in key shortage subjects such as physics and modern languages. Continuous professional development – within and beyond the school, and through joint HMC/GSA arrangements which have led over the years to the current Independent Professional Development (IPD) programme – has grown radically, and since the 1980s there has been far greater emphasis on appraisal and review of performance.

Today's HoD is likely to face annual or two-yearly appraisal by a member of the senior management team (SMT), and then to conduct appraisals of members of his or her department – a process which can be particularly demanding when dealing with colleagues who find the pace of ceaseless changes in syllabuses, module arrangements and examining systems hard to cope with. Advice on career development has become much more systematised: teachers expect it to be given regularly and formally, rather than merely hoping to pick it up themselves by osmosis.

The induction of new teachers (PGCE training, NQTs and ISCTip) and the refreshing of existing ones have become a big part of the HoD's life, as schools have adopted a less top-down approach to in-service training. This approach has also given the HoD a much greater responsibility over the drawing-up and spending of funds, with the growth of devolved departmental budgets. The budgets themselves have grown too, with the arrival of a complete ICT revolution in schools over the past decade, embracing new hardware and software, email, SharePoint systems, and latterly the use of such teaching aids as PowerPoint and SmartBoards.

These, along with more sophisticated science equipment, language laboratories and audio-visual equipment of all types, make every school's ICT requirements one of the hardest areas of expenditure to predict, and its budget one of the most complex to draw up. All of which make the HoD's relationship with the bursar increasingly important.

With the increasing burden of public exams, key stage tests and other forms of assessment right across the school age-range has come, paradoxically, a growing concern that pupils may be insufficiently prepared to practise independent learning, whilst teachers are too often hemmed in by strict syllabus requirements and are tempted to 'teach to the test'. The introduction of inspection, first through the Associations and then via ISI (especially under the models which were in place before ISI 2), put great emphasis on learning styles as well as teaching methods – and forced departments to look at how they delivered their work from first principles.

The scrutiny of departments' work continues: under ISI 2 and its likely successors, the quality of marking and assessment is being rigorously assessed. Inspection looks at a school's results in relation to comparable schools, too (through the so-called 'Turner tables') – something made possible by what might be seen as the biggest change of all which HoDs have had to face: high-profile exam results.

Time was when A level results seemed not to be a particularly big deal. My own results were posted up to Scotland in 1966, where I received them on a Thursday. They had been written with a leaky Biro, and my result in the most important subject was smudged. My reaction was along the lines of: 'Oh well, we'll be home on Tuesday, and perhaps I'll phone the school then'.

There was none of the angst and razzmatazz which now surrounds results day each August as local papers and schools stage photographs of carefully chosen pupils 'celebrating' (sometimes before they have actually been told their results) and journalists make elaborate arrangements with schools to have the data ready for the first edition. Come to think of it, few schools published any public exam results at all in those days, and those that did were regarded as really rather pushy. Parents who asked to see them were seen by many as distinctly vulgar.

Three things dramatically changed all that. First there was the abolition of post-A level Oxbridge Entrance, and the move of all the top universities towards selection by conditional offer, mostly without interview. Secondly, with the gradual growth of the potential student population and increasing concern over fair access, competition for places in selecting universities became much more intense and a subject of much greater public awareness.

And then came league tables. Their introduction in national newspapers early in the 1990s transformed how many schools marketed themselves (in prospectuses and, more latterly, via websites) and how they were perceived by prospective parents. In the process they transformed the role of, and pressures on, the HoD. Suddenly not only could one school be compared with another, but within a school the performance of individual departments could be laid side by side. This process has been underpinned by an explosion in value-added analysis through such mechanisms as MidYIS testing and the ALIS scheme; the modern HoD needs to understand the standard deviations and other statistical concepts which are central to such measurement.

Along with these developments, the HoD's annual review with a member of the senior management team quickly became the norm. Comparatively few independent schools appear to have followed the maintained sector into threshold pay arrangements based on performance, but most teachers know that their results will be noticed and, if necessary, followed up.

Pupils know it too – and can sometimes vote with their feet: for example, when GCSE options subjects have to be chosen in Year 9, or two years later in areas where there are strong sixth form colleges, and staying-on cannot be taken for granted. Day schools recruit hard at both 11+ and 13+ via open days which take place often more than once a year, and boarding schools organise experience days for prep school candidates. The HoD with a busy laboratory or an imaginative piece of locally-based fieldwork may well have a vital role to play in such events.

Finally, there is the role of the HoD in promoting state-independent school partnerships, Academy links and similar schemes, as schools come under increasing pressure to justify their charitable status. Departments in some schools can play a key role in providing opportunities to keep lower-demand subjects alive through local initiatives, and/or providing opportunities for pupils beyond their own school in teacher-shortage subjects such as modern languages and 'hard' sciences.

All the while, the HoD has a vital role to play as the champion of his or her subject – keeping abreast of developments not just in literature but in multi-media resources; keeping the department up-to-date and on-message; and contributing to wider school policy and performance. Thus the head of department, once a role too often filled internally on the principle of seniority or Buggin's Turn, became one which entailed rigorous outside recruitment procedures *and* is now regarded as a crucial part of a successful school's middle management. Read on, and discover in detail how those who have held the role, or who still hold it, view the demands placed on HoDs – and the challenges and job satisfaction which come with them.

Chapter 2

Chief teacher: leading by example

Paul Todd

Becoming a head of department is different from *being* a head of department. You've gone through the long process of ambition, decision and selection, focusing on this outcome above all, and now they've decided to trust you with their precious department. The Head hands you the keys and gets out of the car. You probably know the *big* things you want to change – you'll have discussed them at interview, you'll have dwelt upon them during the vacation – and in the first few weeks you'll address them with energy.

Your recent promotion lends you authority, and the feeling of potency lingers for a while. Some of those planned changes will be welcomed; some will be resisted; some will prove impossible when they clash with reality in the form of lack of time, budgetary considerations, or collective intransigence. That's all part of becoming the head of department, becoming a leader. And what then? What about *being* a leader?

The role of HoD encompasses many things, and only one – a fleeting one, at that – is to be the new broom. Obviously, there are the mechanical things, like responsible budgeting, filling in forms for the director of studies, and reviewing the risk assessments for the classrooms. They simply must be done and, if you're contemplating becoming a head of department, don't underestimate the time they take, or the dullness of some of those chores.

Thankfully, there is a range of less tangible, but more interesting, aspects to the job. Keeping these in mind – when those around you are losing sight of them – is the key to being an outstanding head of department, and to being someone who finds satisfaction and fulfilment in the job. Four of these aspects of leadership are: providing reassurance; establishing a direction; setting the tone; and being a figurehead.

Reassurance is essential, especially at times of change – and when is it *not* a time of change? Anxious parents, insecure members of the SMT, governors keen to get involved – they all need it. And, above all, the teachers and other staff in your department need it, and it's your job to provide it. Reassure them that change will be manageable; consult them; invite their opinions. Reassure them that they are doing a good job, and that their contribution is valued. Reassure everyone by mastery of your subject and familiarity with whole-school issues; by understanding the characteristics and motivations of the staff in your department; by knowing pupils as individuals.

The direction of the department is not an empty mission statement but a crystallisation of the combined educational philosophies of the members of the department. Imposing your own philosophy is less likely to be successful than having an open discussion within the department (possibly over a bottle of wine) after you've been in post for a year or so. What should a pupil have gained by his or her experience in your department? Do you want your department to lead the school in discipline, or in compassion, or in nurturing initiative? Or in a stately progression up the league tables? How do you want pupils to feel when they realise they've got your subject next?

The tone of your department is not easy to identify, let alone change. But it's fun setting about it! You may have already picked up the tone, from attending department meetings, observing lessons, or listening during parents' evenings and casual conversations, or you may need to ask a few questions. Is it vibrant and experimental, or calm and businesslike? Is it inviting? Receptive? Inspiring? What are the energy levels? Do the corridors remind you of an airport, a prison, a hospital or a monastery – not just in their physical appearance, but in the way people behave and talk when passing through?

And the head of a successful department becomes a figurehead, even if you don't set out deliberately to make it so. The reputation of the department reflects your own character. If you're the head of history, you want the director of studies to have the reassurance that history paperwork is completed efficiently; you want the pupils to hear interesting assemblies from the head of history; you want the parents to have the idea that the history teaching is well-orchestrated. You want other new heads of department to be asking if they can look at the history department handbook as an example of good practice.

Those semi-philosophical areas are intriguing, but for a lot of the time they will have to remain in the background. You can't become a full-time philosopher and leave all the teaching to others. The HoD must be an outstanding teacher as well as an administrator and inspirational leader. One of your jobs is to establish high standards, and live by those standards yourself. You might not be able to be the best teacher in *every* aspect of teaching, but the package that a pupil of yours gets should be the best *package*. By now, you should know your own weaknesses, as a teacher, and you have reached a position where you can arrange things so that you compensate for those weaknesses with outstanding strength in other areas.

Your own teaching should continue to improve – it shouldn't get fossilised exactly as it was the day you became HoD. Don't neglect your own INSET, when you're steering people towards training – but make it imaginative. You probably can't stand a day being lectured about classroom management at this stage in your career, but you might find something about problem solving, or lateral thinking, or general leadership.

Ideas from outside the teaching profession can germinate fruitfully in the HoD's mind. It is then your job to pass on these new ideas, both to experienced and to newly-qualified members of the department. They should see you making the effort to keep yourself up-to-date, and they should follow your lead. Make sure, for example, that your colleagues take advantage of conferences and briefing days organised by universities (including their extra-mural departments) on new research – and that they report back to the department on their return.

'Always improving' is a useful target. Remember that some people collect 20 years' experience, while others just have 20 iterations of one year's experience. Take a little time to look for creative ways of improving. For instance, marking, and the feedback you give to pupils after a piece of work, is one area where your habits may have become petrified over the years, but could they be improved – are the pupils getting what they need? What about classroom management – are all the pupils being given the chance to learn in the way that suits them best? Could the classroom be arranged more imaginatively? Is there a type of pupil activity that you've never really tried yet?

Above all, start to *teach* how to teach. If there are young or inexperienced members of staff in the department, time spent talking to them about the mechanics of teaching – however obvious these things may seem to you, at this stage – is never wasted. You never really understand something until you've taught it to someone else, and that is as true of the skills of teaching as it is of the subject material you're now so familiar with. Classroom observation, which means them watching you, not just *you* watching *them*, is a key starting point. All those techniques you've been using to get sixth formers to understand titration, or secondary sources, can now be adapted to get young adults to understand learning styles, differentiation by outcome or peer pressure.

Two particularly good sources of enlightenment, following the mantra of 'always improving', are team-teaching, and the observation of other departments. Team-teaching is a wonderful thing for improving mutual understanding, for injecting some fresh perspective into teachers' approaches, and for opening the students' eyes to the complementary nature of their different teachers' characteristics. Working out a short programme of lesson-observation between two widely different departments – English and physics, say, or art and French – is both invigorating and revealing, a gold-mine of good practice and a glimpse of what the poor pupils have to go through as they rush from English, to physics, to art, to French.

Best of all, perhaps, for refreshing your spirit and getting good ideas, is to spend a day in another school. Most of us are members of regional groups, and it should be fairly easy to agree, with another member of your local group, that you will spend a day in their department, and they will spend a day in yours. This could involve observing (ten minutes of) a number of lessons; sitting in on a department meeting; spending break in the common room; maybe even team-teaching a class with your friend (who would do the same with one of your classes on the return visit). Schools should support absences for this purpose, as the benefit will certainly outweigh the costs.

So, you've settled in, and you'd like to find time to focus on those four aspects of leadership, while leading by example as the best and busiest teacher in the department. How can you possibly fit all that in? It can feel as if you no sooner complete one administrative task, before two more are added to the in-tray.

There is a Japanese term, *karoushi*, which means 'death by overwork'. It has been legally recognised in Japan as a cause of death since the 1980s. Around the end of November or February, many heads of department may feel in danger of succumbing. Are you overworked? Are you working hard enough? Are you lazy or are you obsessive? Everyone strives for some kind of balance between the two extremes. The same idea, wrapped in a fluffier coat, is at the centre of the modern search for 'work-life balance'.

Genuine overwork is a danger we all have to guard against, and talking to people is the best defence. But if you're not, as it were, *clinically* overworked, how do you create some time? With two principal techniques: delegating, and prioritising. Finding the time by forcing yourself to delegate is an issue which all good HoDs think hard about. The reasons for delegation are compelling: to give you time to do the job properly, to give colleagues a chance to develop skills and gain experience, and to get input from the whole team with their varied viewpoints. In addition, the shared workload nurtures community spirit and feelings of collective endeavour.

The reasons why leaders *resist* delegating are usually along the lines of 'if you want something doing right, do it yourself', and 'the others already have enough to do'. These may appear rational at first glance, but frankly they come down to pride – pride in one's own abilities, pride in being a martyr. You're also up against the difficulty of actually asking busy people to take on more work, and we all know it's sometimes easier just to do it yourself – which comes down, frankly, to cowardice.

So you decide that delegation is the right thing to do: how do you go about it? Just give everyone a year-group and ask them to write the scheme of work? The salient point is that people are different. And the sentiment, often attributed to Thomas Jefferson, that 'There is nothing more unequal than the equal treatment of unequal people', applies as much to colleagues as to pupils. Start by identifying the administrative strengths and weaknesses of those in your department – not forgetting yourself. Who is more imaginative (or wayward), who is more punctilious (or nitpicking)? Is *she* better with paperwork and IT, is *he* better with people? Having identified them, though, one can't slavishly adhere to these pre-established strengths; individuals might need to work on their weaknesses, after tactful discussion, for their own career prospects, or for the good of the pupils. So give people tasks which are a good fit with their strengths, but give them a little room to improve too.

In practice, you will have to retain responsibility for budgeting; allocating pupils to sets; the department handbook; department meetings; interviewing and appraising staff; liaison with the SMT; and the monitoring of exam results, take-up, and the workload of the people in your department. But you can delegate costings; and the evaluation of new books or equipment you are considering buying; you can delegate the writing of sections of the handbook and retain editorship; you can delegate liaison with feeder schools and with universities. Someone else can take the minutes of the department meetings (or the task can rotate); someone else can collate internal exam results ready for you to digest.

Jobs which are often delegated, and certainly should be, include writing and reviewing the schemes of work. But there are also setting and marking tests and internal exams; monitoring, updating and managing pupil resources, including on-line ones; running a society or arranging talks; and co-ordinating, and delivering, extra lessons, both remedial and extensional.

Many of these are best handed to a pair of colleagues, or a group of three, if your department is large enough to allow this. The act of delegation must, of course, be accompanied by bolstering comments ("I know you can do this", "I think you're ready to take this on"), and by arrangements to provide support, help and advice ("let's get together next week and we'll see what kind of ideas you've had", "we'll discuss it among the whole department once a month and they can all feed their ideas to you").

There are some areas for which the whole department should take collective responsibility. One thinks of the selection of a new syllabus, but also of things which improve your group morale, such as bringing in biscuits, arranging a department dinner or going out for a drink together. Another good idea is to relieve the bureaucracy by devoting an occasional department meeting to "everyone describing something that's worked well recently" or "your turn to teach us all, for 15 minutes, anything of your choice, as if we were pupils". Take it in turns to present ideas on how to teach the most difficult topics, with everyone playing their part. It's everyone's responsibility to make sure the department meetings are as beneficial as they can be, but it's your responsibility to make sure the others know that.

Finding the time means prioritising. The latter – the equivalent of medical triage – is another 'obvious' requirement which is rarely given the thought it needs. Creative prioritising can make all the difference between a manager who manages, and a manager who excels. One very useful technique in creative triage is identifying the little things which have big effects – and then making sure you do them.

Perhaps the most important is thanking people. The positive results of a handwritten thank-you note, or a comment showing that you noticed the success of some venture, are out of all proportion to the time involved. The same goes for offering sincere good wishes, going out of your way to give a warm greeting, and enquiring about a recent family illness. These will be appreciated by those whom you work with, whatever their role and perceived status in the organisation from the highest to the lowest. They will help others to have a positive view of you, too: there is a good deal of truth in the old saying that you should 'judge a man by how he treats his inferiors'.

Yes, it might take a little research before you know the details and can congratulate a colleague in an informed and authentic way on his or her successes, but it will repay you tenfold. And time spent popping in to give a smile and a greeting is never wasted. Never forget, either, that many of the people with whom we work possess skills that we shall never have – and that some of them have none of the future prospects that we enjoy.

In the administration of the department, there are probably ten or 20 ways in which you can make life easier for others with just a few minutes of effort. Find them, use them – they will be noticed. For example, I remember that when distributing large charts of internal exam results to housemasters, I would use a highlighter to emphasise the names of the pupils in each house, because without that assistance the relevant names were lost in a welter of eight-point *sans serif*. A moment spent with a highlighter, to personalise a sheaf of photocopies, is a moment well spent.

The people best described as your 'inferiors' are, inevitably, the pupils. Knowing every single pupil might be beyond the best of us. But if you devote a little time to identifying the weakest ones, the very able ones, and the victims of life's vicissitudes, so that you can pick them out for a supportive remark in the corridor or the lunch queue, and discuss them in an informed way with their teachers, not only will you do these pupils a great service, but it will be noticed by their pastoral carers and their parents – and you will get a well-earned reputation for knowing the pupils as individuals.

The other side of the same coin, and equally valuable when prioritising, is identifying the *big* things that have *little* effects. Sadly, you won't find many time-consuming tasks which are universally admitted to be of little value, but there will be some which eat up more hours than they justify. This is a personal thing, because something which *you* do quickly might take someone else much longer – you might have a weakness with numbers, with grammar, or with IT. In these tasks, find short-cuts which bring you *nearly* all the benefit for a fraction of the time.

Budgeting might well be an area where time savings can be made without any actual risk of going over-budget (for that's what really matters); asking another head of department to check your sums while you check their spelling might save time. Invigilation, supervision of play-time, sitting on a bus going to a fixture or a museum – review those things, and see if you can be creative in getting more out of the minutes you spend on things like that.

Allied to this is the importance of using the resources available. Ask for advice. There are other heads of department to ask, and usually there will be an ex-head of department or two available for a chat. Everyone loves being asked for advice, and ex-heads of department, it sometimes seems, live for it. Swallow your pride, and force yourself to ask.

Ask for help, ask for cover – will the school cover your Year 7 class so you can team-teach with your inexperienced but energetic colleague? You won't know unless you ask. Does the school have an enlightened view of the benefits of reading weeks, of study days, of keeping their managers fresh? In my school we have separate (and generous) budgets for mini-sabbaticals (usually around six weeks) and reading weeks. There is often some direct training benefit, around which the time is planned, but not necessarily – sometimes the benefit is simply through refreshing the member of staff, though this does not make the benefit less real.

The top priority is not always the obvious one. You are timetabled to teach three groups on 6th May, but you, your pupils and your school might benefit more if you spend that day on the sort of intellectual refreshment described above as being part of 'leading by example'. Study days are a prime example of days rarely ill-spent; many universities have facilities for teachers to spend some study time on campus, making use of library facilities and so on. An enlightened school will include this as an INSET option, and if you've never explored that sort of possibility, you're not being very creative.

Other aspects of creative triage are extra-curricular participation, and personal 'hinterland'. Extra-curricular work usually involves games, pastoral work, or clubs and activities. It is not desirable to drop out of these three things when you become a head of department – in fact, I recommend trying to take on a little of each, even if you've never done so before. Games and sports, it is widely recognised, give you invaluable insights into the wider school and the lives of the students. True, games practices and fixtures are time-consuming, so sharing the commitment with another head of department might be best. But getting out of your corridor into a different environment, getting some exercise, and seeing colleagues and pupils in a semi-recreational way, are worth the time for most of us.

Pastoral work, such as tutoring or involvement with some club or evening activity, brings similar benefits. But take care over two things: first, you should by now be able to ensure that you are doing things you *enjoy* when it comes to games and activities, at least most of the time; and, second, don't try to take command of these areas. Being head of department is enough. In busy schools, we all have a lot of hats to wear, and only one of your hats should have 'boss' written on it. So, by all means help with a rugby team, but don't try to be in charge of it; be a house tutor, but leave the big decisions to the housemaster; accompany the Duke of Edinburgh's Award expeditions but subordinate yourself deliberately and to whomever is nominally in charge.

By 'hinterland', in a professional context, I mean your life outside work, and especially your intellectual life. Ultimately, your family should always come first – especially in the holidays, on Sundays, or whenever its nearest and dearest members suddenly need you, and the school should recognise that. But at other times it may sometimes take a conscious decision to raise its priority in your long list of current preoccupations. Every individual has the right to have preferences and priorities in life, but it would be short-sighted to pay no attention to your own physical health, to your friends, or to your intellectual development.

The hectic pace of term-time, followed by the relatively long spells of holiday, mean that we in education do not find it easy to get into a routine of exercise or gym visits. However, in all seriousness, ignoring the need for exercise is as negligent as driving when tired, or slipping towards alcoholism – other serious matters to which highly-stressed individuals are vulnerable. If you can't find time for exercise; if you can't find time to read a new book; if you can't find time for your friends; something is awry. It's facile to say that, while you have a professional responsibility to the school, your first responsibility is to yourself; but it's certainly true that, if you neglect your responsibility to yourself, you won't be doing the school any good either.

Like all 'promoted positions', being a head of department is not an easy life: it's no sinecure. There's very little lying on couches being fed grapes by handmaidens, even in the best-run departments. What looks like power from the outside can often feel only like responsibility from the inside. So here are three things to remember if the burden feels oppressive and the days seem dark.

First, remember that you chose this. In saying that, I'm not casting you into some 'You made your bed, now lie in it' dungeon. On the contrary – the point is that you made that choice, and you can make other choices in the future. Educated people with management experience have lots of options. You are an impressive and competent person and, each day, you are choosing to do this job, like a good existentialist. Don't feel trapped – feel empowered by the fact that you've got yourself here.

Secondly, remember the holidays! This sounds flippant but is utterly serious: it's so easy to forget, at the end of November, how wonderful the job is in July and August, or even in May when the pupils are revising and you have time to fit everything in comfortably. All the pupils and staff get tired and irritable together towards the ends of the long terms, and we so easily bring each other down, our despondent mood growing as the positive energy reserves in the common room become exhausted. Recognise this, and rise above it.

Thirdly, and most importantly, remember that everything, everything you do, does some good. It's so easy to forget. Every bit of praise or advice you give a pupil, every cheerful remark to a colleague, every expression of appreciation to a subordinate. Pupils, and indeed younger staff, *do* observe what you do; they do hear what you say; and they often notice it to an astonishing degree. Pupils will tell you, 20 years after leaving the school, what an impact some remark had upon them. Yes, you have responsibility, but it's the responsibility that comes from having significant influence over a lot of people at the time in their lives when they are most in need of positive influence. Just think of all the good you can do, and then go out and do it.

Chapter 3

Monitoring the effectiveness of the department's work

Jane Gandee

When I became a head of department, I don't remember discussing at the interview how I intended to monitor the work of the members of my department. Rather, I spent much time rhapsodising about my love for my subject, about inspiring both students and colleagues and about leading by example. I certainly believed that it was essential to run an effective department, but I rather ingenuously supposed that my new colleagues would simply recognise the obvious good sense of my many innovative suggestions and fall into line.

'Ide-ALIS-ts' aside, there are other heads of department who see themselves primarily as good classroom teachers who are prepared to spend a little more time than their colleagues organising the department's resources, choosing a new exam board or attending INSET. They do not feel that they are directly responsible for the teaching and learning in their department or for the exam results.

However, why be head of department if you are not prepared to take responsibility for what goes on in your subject area? And if you are going to be responsible for the achievements of your department, you will have to monitor the work of your colleagues. Even when HoDs accept that they should take responsibility for exam results and so on, they often baulk at the idea of monitoring their colleagues, the argument being that such behaviour indicates a lack of trust.

However, monitoring can be a way of protecting and supporting them. Take Mr X, the serial complainant. When he contacts the school to say that his son's teacher frequently loses homework and cannot control the class, you will easily be able to rebut these claims if you have regularly observed lessons and carried out work scrutinies. Moreover it is more than likely that, during your monitoring, you will see some extremely good practice on which you will be able to congratulate colleagues.

It is hard to imagine any other profession that would not have some form of quality assurance carried out on a regular basis. The annual analysis of exam results – whilst important – is not really enough on its own. More regular monitoring is essential. Although I have already touched on lesson observations and work scrutiny, it seems to me that the key to achieving an effective department is to invest time in establishing shared standards and expectations.

In the past, HoDs, and indeed directors of studies, often assumed that everyone knew what was meant by 'good teaching' or 'marking'. Before the advent of league tables it perhaps didn't particularly matter if that wasn't the case and if one person's idea of good teaching was to talk for 40 minutes without drawing breath, while another's was to spend most of the lesson talking about his time in the Army. Of course it mattered to students, but they tended to be a largely disenfranchised part of the educational process.

Few members of the teaching profession are unambiguously in favour of league tables but, if these tables have encouraged middle and senior managers to look more closely at the quality and consistency of teaching and learning within their schools, they have been of service. A first step in the monitoring of any department's work must be for the members of that department to come together to thrash out a number of issues. They will want to discuss at least some of the following: teaching methodology; what is set for homework; assessment techniques; expectations relating to the behaviour of students; teaching and learning techniques; expectations and targets and getting feedback from students.

There is little point in setting up a programme of monitoring if some members of the department are unaware of departmental norms and expectations. Once these have been agreed, the role of the HoD is to check that everyone is doing what they said they would. Although this could be construed as 'checking up' on colleagues, in departments and schools with the right sort of collaborative atmosphere, monitoring should be embraced as an opportunity for teachers to 'show off' good practice, refresh their understanding of the aims of their department and reflect on their own practice.

MidYIS, ALIS, value added, Fischer Family Trust, Morrisby, standardised residuals, scattergrams and so on all have pros and cons. It can be very easy to draw up complicated charts, analyse results by teaching set, by gender, by unit, and still come up with absolutely nothing of any statistical significance. The problem for many independent schools is that samples are often so small that one student performing particularly well or particularly badly will skew the results, giving a value added score that does not reflect accurately a particular teacher's diligence and effectiveness.

On the other hand, both MidYIS and ALIS value added scores can sometimes be valuable in providing evidence to confirm suspicions that you already have. However, this is more likely to happen at whole school (rather than departmental) level unless you teach in a particularly large school with a large ability range. A curriculum manager is far more likely to have his/her suspicions confirmed about the indifferent teaching of, let's say, the history department, than a HoD is to discover that one of his/her teachers is underperforming. Over time one might gather enough data to show that progress in a particular teacher's set is markedly worse or better than in other classes, but this is by no means certain.

I have gradually come to the view that MidYIS baseline scores and GCSE predictions are best used in conjunction with other measures, such as end of year exams, to check that students are making appropriate progress. Heads of department will want to track students over time. Best practice would probably involve some sort of spreadsheet showing MidYIS baseline scores, marks from any standardised end of unit tests set across the year group and results from end of year exams.

Depending on how your school operates, it might also include periodic progress grades. It would show movement from one year to the next, so that it would be possible to see which students had made more progress than the rest (perhaps moving from 50th to 20th over the course of one academic year) and which had made less progress. Referring back to entrance exam scores in schools which have an academically selective entry can sometimes be revealing, too.

It is also useful to look at the end of year exam results by teaching group. If the teaching groups are mixed ability and one class gets significantly better results than the others, what does this tell you? Did the teacher of that class give the students too much information about the exam? Or too specific a revision schedule? If you want to guarantee consistency, you will need to ensure that the teacher setting the exam issues a revision sheet that goes to every student sitting the exam and that teachers do not elaborate on this.

If preparation for the exam was the same in every teaching set, then what is the teacher with the better results doing that other teachers are not? What can all colleagues learn about motivation, engagement, rigour *etc*? Equally, if one class's results are markedly lower, what does that tell the HoD about the teacher? What can you deduce (or what should you *resist* the temptation to deduce), about the quality of teaching to a group whose members all score their lowest A level grade in your department's subject? These things may tell you nothing that you don't already know, but how do you then deal with the problems for the next academic year? At least the exam results give you something concrete on which to base a discussion.

If your monitoring sheet reveals students who are underperforming, you will want to discuss them as a department and decide on an appropriate course of action – such as inviting them to attend clinics, assigning them a sixth form mentor, contacting their parents/form teacher/housemaster/housemistress, arranging for them to set aside time each week to do your particular subject's homework, seating them in a different place in class, setting them specific holiday homework *etc*.

Equally, if you see that a student has performed well, you will want to recognise success in some way. Whatever your preferred method of commending or chastising, you will want to make sure that it is consistently applied by all involved. There is nothing more counter-productive and guaranteed to make people ignore you in the future than instituting a system and failing to ensure that it is followed.

When using ALIS, once again it is probably best to use the predicted grades merely as guidelines rather than as target grades. While MidYIS can produce GCSE predictions that are rather low, ALIS predictions will tend to be rather high if you are working in a school that has good value-added at GCSE. This is because the GCSE grades are used to generate A level predictions and these GCSE grades have already been maximised by high expectations, good teaching *etc* at that level.

It is, however, also possible for students to sit a baseline test, which will again generate predicted A level grades. In this case I have found that predictions are rather lower because they reflect the innate ability of the students without taking account of things such as work ethic. The dilemma then is what to do with the two contrasting sets of predictions.

The higher set sometimes leads teachers to mistrust the whole ALIS system as they tend to be unrealistic for those students who peaked at GCSE. However, the lower set based on apparent innate ability can be too unchallenging. The University of Durham itself uses the predictions based on GCSE results to produce its value added data as it has found that these results are the best predictors of A level performance.

Once the students' progress has been monitored, the HoD will probably turn his/her attention to teaching and learning. One of the most obvious ways to do this is through lesson observations. It is undeniably far easier to create a climate in which observations are an everyday occurrence if the senior management team decree that this should be the case. It is considerably more challenging as a HoD to create the only department in the school in which staff are regularly observed, however important you feel it is that such observations should take place.

It is vital to be absolutely clear about the function of lesson observations. There are many processes which involve annual lesson observations, such as the school appraisal system, but these very often lack focus. No-one knows why they are taking place other than to satisfy the demands of a particular system. No-one knows what will be concluded once the observation is over or how the observation fits into any department (or school) wide policy.

If you, as HoD, are going to introduce observations as part of your drive to monitor and improve teaching quality, you will first need to decide *why* you should observe lessons, and then you will decide who observes and how frequently. Finally, it is crucial to know what to do with the data thus gathered. Again you will have discussed with your department important issues such as what you all mean by 'good teaching', or how you can encourage students to be more independent or how you might improve your questioning techniques, and these will be some of the things that you want to check on when you are observing.

Whilst it is obviously good practice to use the ISI lesson observation form when the school is about to be inspected, you might find it more useful to devise your own form to reflect the aspects of teaching and learning on which you want to concentrate. Ideally this would be drawn up in consultation with all members of the department so that everyone is reminded about what the department considers to be important when it comes to teaching and learning.

Once everyone knows what is expected of them in the classroom you will need to observe them in action. The ideal frequency of lesson observations is a moot point and once again it is helpful if some sort of edict comes from the senior management team. Once a year might usefully be taken as a minimum, but of course it could depend on the members of your department.

What should you do with the data being collected? One suggestion that I have taken from *Managing subject departments for pupil achievement* by Steve Rowe (Heinemann, 2000), is to compile an anonymous sheet on which the things that you would like to see happening in lessons, such as increased 'wait time', are listed on the left. After the first lesson observation, in column one, a 'blob' or tick is placed against each activity observed. After the second lesson observation the same thing happens (in column two) and so on until all the proposed lesson observations are complete. This gives patterns for the department as a whole and shows what, if anything, needs to be emphasised before the next round of lesson observations. Obviously for small departments anonymity cannot be assured, so it could be worth teaming up with another subject area.

Pupil voice initiatives seek to involve students in decision-making in every aspect of school life. Although some teachers will be horrified at the idea of asking students about their teaching, it seems to me entirely sensible to seek feedback from the consumer, regardless of age. There are several commercial systems which allow you to question students about the quality of teaching and learning or about the classroom environment.

MidYIS, for example, offers a questionnaire that asks students about their attitudes to a number of different subjects. This questionnaire could be adapted to give information about particular teaching sets. However, I am unconvinced that this type of 'top down' approach to student voice is the best one. The reason for seeking feedback from students is to improve one's own teaching, so students' opinions need to be sought as soon as a particular topic or activity has been completed. Their views can then inform lesson planning for the next unit of work. In this way students feel listened to and the teacher can quickly improve anything that is not working.

Perhaps the most challenging aspect of *pupil voice* is encouraging those teachers who most need feedback to get involved. It seems inevitable that those teachers who are willing to seek the opinions of their students are almost by definition those who least need to modify their teaching methods. The challenge therefore is how to encourage other teachers to take part. Although leading by example never does any harm, it can also be a good idea to ask a member of the management team to congratulate someone publicly on getting involved in *pupil voice*. Alternatively, a member of staff who has enjoyed feedback from students can be encouraged to talk about the process (loudly and enthusiastically) in the staff room at break time. This can persuade other colleagues to get involved.

In many schools, looking at students' books is very far from being part of the culture. However, it is an extremely simple and effective way of raising standards, ensuring effective teaching and learning and of initiating conversations about important issues such as assessment, differentiation and expectations. You might want to launch a work scrutiny in the wake of a new initiative, such as Assessment for Learning, as a way of checking that everyone is using comment-only marking; or you might decide to do a work scrutiny as a way of beginning a review of assessment within your subject area. Depending on the composition of your department, it might once again be easiest to launch such an initiative if it is something upon which the entire school is focused. Remember too that work scrutiny is a growing feature of school inspection.

Whatever the rationale for your decision to carry out a work scrutiny, you will want to decide on a particular year group and then select some students from the top, middle and bottom of the ability range within the year group. You will also want to make sure that these students are taught by a variety of different teachers. It is then up to you to decide the focus of your work scrutiny.

The assumption tends to be that a work scrutiny will always concentrate on assessment, but it could also examine progress. Is the work set in the middle of the year more demanding than the work set at the beginning of the year? Does students' work seem to be improving as the year progresses, or do writing and presentation improve or worsen over time? Do the same mistakes occur at the end of the year as at the beginning of the year? Is work set in Year 8 more demanding than work set in Year 7? And so on.

A scheme of work should be a working document: something to which both you and members of your department refer on a regular basis. Should you fall under a bus, it will allow your replacement to continue teaching with the same pace and coverage that you employ. It will refer to teaching and learning techniques and indicate assessment opportunities.

It will have links to resources stored on the school's virtual learning environment and it will have prompts to remind you what to set for homework and when to set it. In short, as teachers always say to students planning an essay, once the plan is complete you can stop thinking and get on with executing it. A carefully thought-out and detailed scheme of work means that you do not have to spend too much time before each lesson wondering what you are going to do. Furthermore, assuming that everyone sticks to it, a scheme of work ensures consistent delivery in the form of the highest common denominator.

This is not to say that teachers cannot bring an individual style to the delivery of their lessons. The best schemes of work are likely to contain an element of 'must' and 'could' so that individual teachers can, to a certain extent, choose what to deliver and how. A scheme of work is not simply the contents list of your textbook with dates by each item. For example, you will want to decide what you expect all students to be able to do by the end of Year 7 in your subject area. You will probably also want to plot what some students will be able to do. It is likely that you will look at both content and process. You will include extension activities for your gifted and talented students.

The scheme of work will be a working document to be reviewed at the end of each academic year. It should by this stage be covered with notes and suggestions. You will need to decide how to ensure that all members of your department feel a sense of ownership and actually follow it. How do you convince the maverick teacher of 25 years' experience whose results are always excellent that (s)he should stick to the same scheme of work as the rest of the department? Does it matter if (s)he doesn't?

Differentiation can be thought of as both the Holy Grail and the *bête noire* of teaching. If one is not to be driven to an early grave by trying to produce differentiated activities for 20 or more individuals, it is crucial to plan ahead and to be 're-ALIS-tic'. This is where the scheme of work should come into its own. It should include links to materials for those who need more support and for those who need more challenging work.

In addition it should suggest some activities that differentiate. It is clearly a waste of time for each individual teacher to try to come up with differentiated materials before each lesson when these could have been prepared as a team effort at the beginning of the year. This does not preclude the production of further activities throughout the year as the scheme of work should always be a working document, but it does lessen the burden and once again ensures that every teacher will be able to cater for a range of abilities within his/her class.

It is surprising how often teachers talk about teaching able students 'beyond the syllabus' and of setting extension work, both of which on closer examination turn out to be simply more of the same. Able students do not want more of the same; that is hardly a reward for working well.

On the contrary, they need less of the same. If (in French) an average pupil needs to do ten questions on the imperfect tense in order to understand it well enough to incorporate in essays, a more able pupil will need to do fewer questions in order to gain a clear understanding. And then what does (s)he do? Certainly not more questions on a topic which has already been mastered.

There is much advice available on gifted and talented, both subject-specific and more general, and it is likely that your school will have some sort of gifted and talented policy. In many schools a conscious decision is taken not to identify gifted and talented students formally, but rather to seek to raise the achievement of all pupils by offering a range of opportunities both inside and outside the classroom.

After all, a high achiever in one subject area may not be a high achiever in another and the level of achievement will vary from lesson to lesson. A gifted writer of imaginative essays may not be a gifted debater. Regardless of your school's policy, you will probably still need to decide on activities suitable for those students who, on any given day, grasp new concepts more quickly than their peers. The activities must be readily available so that teachers do not have to resort to setting students 'more of the same'.

If students are set within your subject area, you might opt for letting some take their GCSE at the end of Year 10 (or earlier). However, it can then be difficult to decide what students should do in Year 11. In general I think that they should have the opportunity to learn new skills (for example, starting an additional language) and do more challenging activities rather than taking yet another GCSE, which will essentially be no more challenging than the exam they have just sat. Yet, it may not necessarily be in their best interests to take an AS exam, as they are already overburdened with assessment.

Outside the classroom, running enrichment activities within your subject area will attract students to your department and help to raise its profile. In addition, they will be engaging and challenging for students. You might want to consider a subject-specific club; subject-related trips; assemblies organised by students; a newsletter; an inter-house competition; older students running clinics/mentoring sessions for younger students; students entering inter-school competitions; a reading group or a weekly quiz question for your school newsletter or to be displayed on a notice board – which might also feature news stories related to your subject area chosen by students; material for display screens organised by students; debates/discussions on a subject-specific issue; inviting speakers into school *etc.*

There are many possibilities that will encourage students to use what they have learnt in the classroom in a wider context. Seize them whenever and wherever you can!

Chapter 4

Leading and managing your staff

Michael Carslaw

It is often said that you can lead a horse to water but you can't make it drink – a not infrequent cry from those in the middle tier of leadership/management in a busy independent school. Who are the leaders in this instance? For that matter, who are the followers? Heads of department will fit into both categories in different contexts.

For them, as with all teachers, time is a most precious commodity. There simply never seems to be enough of it. So how can they do all the things they are supposed to do? Manage and lead staff who may often have a range of other responsibilities and/or may be reluctant to do what the HoD wants? Appraise their performance and make sure that they are taking their continuous professional development (CPD) seriously? And keep staff on task – even though there may be other things that they would much rather be doing?

Napoleon Bonaparte described leaders (and, yes, heads of department *are* leaders) as 'dealers in hope'. Given this, how can HoDs bring hope to those around them and produce the outcomes which their Head is expecting from them?

HoDs have essentially three options. First, they can focus solely on a number of outcomes – for example GCSE/GCE exam results – and judge the success of their and their department's performance purely in terms of the achievement (or otherwise) of these outcomes. Such HoDs, by and large, allow the teachers in their department to get on with things and, as long as the results look good every August, leave them alone.

The teachers in this imaginary department are made up of the 'unconsciously competent' – in other words highly professional at their job but functioning on a form of auto-pilot. All well and good when things are going well – but beware when change is in the air (for example, when there is a major change in specification; or the academic profile of the school changes; or when an inspection is looming). When that happens, the 'unconsciously competent' can quickly become the 'unconsciously incompetent'.

The second option is to leave teachers alone no matter *what* the results are. Such HoDs view themselves as administrators, not leaders or even managers, intent solely on making sure the department is suitably stocked and timetables are fairly allocated. 'It's the Head's responsibility to appoint the staff and I'll leave them to get on with it'. The teachers in this kind of department could be unconsciously competent, but there is also quite a high chance that they will be unconsciously incompetent and disaster is almost inevitable.

The third option is to take the best aspects of the former category – taking a keen interest in outcomes, but also taking a leadership role in the implementation of the various skills, processes and practices that make an excellent department. HoDs who take this option will find that their empire is populated by the 'consciously competent': practitioners who are aware that pupils aren't the only individuals doing the learning, because the teachers are doing so as well.

They are what Donald Schön describes as 'reflective practitioners'. In addition, it's not just teachers who are learning from other teachers, but also departments learning from other departments, or schools learning from other schools or organisations. These departments or schools can be viewed as what Andy Hargreaves calls 'professional learning communities' and what Peter Senge defines as 'learning organisations'.

I think it makes sense to refer to these categories as anti-managerialists, a-managerialists and managerialists respectively. Managerialism is often used as a pejorative term but if combined with a view that leadership is an important part of being a HoD and if it takes into account the values of the school, it is helpful in focusing the attention of the HoD on the skills, processes and practices that make a good department even better. It also provides a sustainable model on which successful audits of performance can be made by means of teacher performance review or appraisal.

What are these skills, processes and practices going to be? The main focus of a good HoD is always going to be the quality of teaching and learning in his or her department. Such HoDs' attention should constantly be drawn (if not by themselves, then by their senior managers or teachers in their departments) to good skills, processes and practices that are going to enable teachers in the department to teach effectively. We need to take all sorts of factors into account: what a good lesson looks like; how children learn; stretching the most able; effective approaches to marking and reporting; using ICT to maximum benefit in the classroom; making good use of ALIS and MiDYIS data and so on.

How can a HoD help teachers in the department to develop these skills, processes and practices? Here the importance of high quality CPD is paramount. Different HoDs will have different approaches to CPD; for anti-managerialists and a-managerialists, it is a matter of indifference: teachers will simply get on and find out about whatever they feel they need to find out about. For the anti-managerialist, as long as they come up with the required exam results, there is not much to be concerned about.

However, effective HoDs value the importance of scholarship underpinned by the skills, processes and practices that lead to good teaching and learning. For them, CPD is critical in helping to create and maintain the culture of learning within the department – and not just the learning done by pupils in the classroom. Effective CPD does not just mean going on an expensive and often wasteful course – though many are very valuable, notably the excellent IPD programme.

The limitations of CPD are in part a constraint brought on by the requirements of ISI inspection. CPD itself has a relatively low level of importance and rarely features as a significant issue of comment in the final inspection report. However the impact of good CPD, coupled with high levels of knowledge sharing among teachers (delivered for example by means of in-house training sessions) can have a disproportionately positive impact on the quality of teaching and learning. Unlike CPD itself, this is perceived as having a high level of importance and will attract much comment in any inspection report.

How can these tensions be resolved? A widely used process is teacher performance review – or appraisal – which takes on many guises in the independent sector. This is rightly so. The sector celebrates its diversity and this leads to different expectations of teachers – particularly when the sector takes a holistic view of the child, and not just one defined in the state sector as a deliverer of targets. However at the core of performance review is the focus on effective teaching and learning.

Unfortunately teacher performance review has a poor record in the independent sector, as I discovered whilst doing some research in 1998. Schools in the '90s typically introduced a performance review scheme when inspection was close (chart 1). Such schemes run for one or maybe two cycles, before falling into disrepair and being reinvigorated only when the next inspection is in sight.

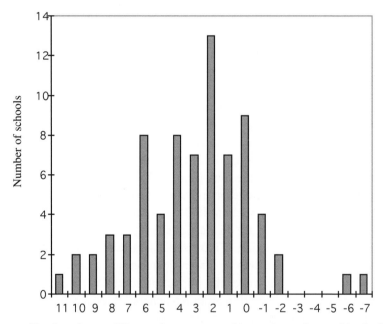

Number of years difference between year of inspection and year of institution.
Positive values indicate inspection occurring after institution of appraisal scheme.
Negative values indicate the reverse.

Chart 1, showing the association between year of inspection and year of institution of appraisal scheme (HMC schools only).

The reason for this is that the effectiveness of performance review is closely associated with the nature of the teacher culture in any given school. Performance review is by its nature a process; and if the teachers in that school – however apparently good – are essentially anti-managerialist or a-managerialist in nature and outlook, it will in all probability fail, because it will be perceived by the teachers concerned as an irrelevant process.

The key point here is that the nature of the performance review scheme and its sustainability in any given school are strong indicators of the nature of teacher culture within that school. What is the nature of teacher culture in your department or school? How would you classify it? Managerialist, anti-managerialist or a-managerialist?

Having said this, how can performance review be made sustainable and effective? Many schools have responded by calling their performance review scheme anything but appraisal (professional development review; performance management; performance development; performance review for professional development *etc*). However this fails to convince when the intention of the scheme (as often exemplified in its title) fails to match up with the reality of its implementation.

Why is this so difficult? The key tension leading to failure, and which a good HoD needs to recognise if not resolve, is between the use of a performance review as a summative tool to audit current performance and as a formative tool to enable performance to improve in the future. This raises in itself a number of issues. What is the nature of a teacher's performance? How can it be audited?

In most independent schools, unlike some in the state sector, job tasks performed by a teacher fall into three categories. The most important involves teaching and learning in the classroom (this should be obvious, but for a few it isn't – particularly in a busy school with a lot going on); the second involves pastoral responsibilities (which can take the form of being a tutor, or housemaster or housemistress or year head *etc*); the third category is contribution to the co-curriculum, for example on the games field, Duke of Edinburgh's Award *etc*).

Given this, teachers can be pulled in three ways by three different line managers – all making time demands. In addition the status of each of the line managers can vary. For example, in many schools, the middle managers with the highest status are the housemasters and housemistresses who have a pastoral responsibility and for whom classroom teaching may be a necessary distraction. The status of these individuals is often higher than the poor old HoD, who nominally line manages someone with a greater status – not an easy task.

This makes it essential that HoDs have clear job descriptions, as well as a clear understanding of the job descriptions of the teachers who make up their department, whether a housemaster or housemistress, master in charge of the first XV rugby or whatever. As a head of department have you seen the job descriptions of your department members? Who is the most important line manager for each (for a housemaster/housemistress it may well be a deputy head – not you)?

Once job descriptions are clear, it is then possible to make a summative audit of performance as well as the outcomes. A key audit will be external exam performance, whether GCSE, A levels or Common Entrance *etc*. This in itself will be an almost totally sufficient measure for anti-managerialists. However effective, HoDs will want to look further, scrutinising how teachers work and what skills, processes and practices they are using.

Here lesson observation is vital and there are some excellent resources available to help, for instance Sara Bubb and Peter Earley, *Leading and Managing Continuing Professional Development: Developing People, Developing Schools*, (Paul Chapman publishing/Sage, 2007): a particularly valuable reference in placing observation in the context of effective CPD – though the effective HoD will want to pay attention not just to the quality of teaching, but also to aspects such as the quality of marking, report writing, and effective use of rewards and sanctions.

A critical decision to be faced is whether to rank lessons (for example using ISI guidelines to assess whether a lesson is outstanding, good, satisfactory *etc*) and/or to use observations as an opportunity to focus on particular aspects of teaching and learning. The former is associated with the summative aspects of performance review; the latter with the more developmental formative aspects.

HoDs additionally need to be wary of the dangers of using performance review as part of a disciplinary procedure against a particular teacher: if this is done, performance review takes on a much less formative and developmental nature and becomes a highly judgmental process (despite whatever is said about the developmental objectives of the scheme as articulated by the SMT or others). However, apparent underperformance in such circumstances should not be a surprise to the observant HoD and the performance review of the teacher should reflect this.

Once the performance audit is completed, it is possible to move on to the more transformational and formative aspects of performance review which involve the CPD of your staff. This is probably the most difficult aspect for an anti-managerialist teacher or HoD to come to terms with, focusing as it does on the skills, processes and practices that can invigorate a department: stimulating a jaded teacher; pushing on a young enthusiast looking for a first promotion and providing opportunities for a HoD to show leadership and initiative. Being as paper light and user-friendly as possible helps considerably and I would encourage HoDs to go for a short cycle (one year?) snappy and effective process.

Effective CPD can take many forms: making presentations to colleagues; observing other teachers; finding out what is happening in other schools; making networks; even casual conversations with colleagues. Effective HoDs and the teachers in their department need to embark on a constant and relentless quest to explore and research; adapt and innovate; refine and hone. This is coupled with an eagerness to share knowledge, not just within departments but also between them as well (for example by observation of teachers in other departments) and between different schools.

All schools will impose a certain number of processes and practices on teachers by means of policies (for instance, a marking and assessment policy and a rewards and sanctions policy). However, it is comparatively unusual in the independent sector to find departments which go beyond the basic implementation of such policies and share knowledge in a way that does make a difference to the quality of teaching and learning – however good that teaching and learning may already be.

How effective is the CPD provision in your school? Is it a matter of sending a colleague on a course or is it much more deeply embedded in the teacher culture? How do you evaluate CPD in your department and how do you know that it has an impact on teaching and learning? What opportunities do teachers have to deliver training themselves? How does it inform your departmental development plan or in turn is informed by it? Is it top-down or bottom-up?

Once a particular teacher culture is embedded in a department, it becomes easier to use performance review to audit performance and secure improvement by means of effective CPD. It is difficult, if not impossible, to change teacher culture *solely* by means of performance review – and particularly if the performance review scheme stresses the importance of professional development and sharing knowledge to cynical anti-managerialists.

Given this, what can a HoD do to lead and motivate colleagues? One widely used tool is the use of targets to improve performance. Again there have been interesting changes in the forms of words used by schools and organisations to describe a target to be set for an adult – for example as an objective or an intent. As a result, the process risks becoming progressively more blurred.

Effective targets are usually described as being SMART (sensible, measurable, achievable, realistic and time-limited is one expansion of the acronym – though I have come across at least five others). But as Mark Rose has written, they do have the danger of being DUMB (defective, unreliable, misdirected or meaningless and bureaucratic). If this can be avoided, targets can have considerable value when used sensitively and appropriately and not excessively (five per year at the very most; ideally three).

High levels of interpersonal and leadership skills are required if targets are to work – a skill lacking in many middle managers, particularly when dealing with a cynical anti-managerialist or the busy housemaster who would rather be doing something else. HoDs also need to recognise that targets will have different meanings for different teachers – and clarity is vital.

A structural difficulty in many schools' schemes occurs for an effective HoD keen on using performance review, knowledge sharing and CPD well, when (s)he does not have the lead role in coordinating the appraisal of an individual teacher, because that responsibility is taken by someone of a higher status. This significantly disempowers the

HoD and marginalises his or her capacity for leadership considerably – the HoD's input into any given teacher's targets being limited and reduced in value. However, this is not necessarily a problem if the overarching culture in the school is anti-managerialist or a-managerialist – but it is a major difficulty.

How many targets does your school's performance review scheme set for each teacher? How many of them are related to teaching and learning? Who drives the performance review process in your department? Is it you or the teacher or a more senior person? How are targets monitored (one study showed that teachers had little recollection of their targets three months after their appraisal)?

High levels of interpersonal and leadership skills are also required in using rewards to motivate staff. School-wide rewards such as a form of performance-related pay (PRP) are not widely used in the independent sector – again a reflection of a more holistic view of a teacher's performance that is not shared so widely with the state sector.

If PRP is used, the performance review process becomes immediately more judgmental and less developmental in nature: hard cash is now involved. So HoDs can reward teachers in other ways – the reward being the quality of the department; its facilities; the departmental area; relationships between colleagues (those interpersonal skills again). All are factors which make a department a pleasant (though not complacent) and challenging place of work.

Two final key questions: what can you do, as a head of department, to reward your colleagues for doing well? How are you building your team and preparing it for success? In summary, being a head of department is one of the most rewarding jobs an individual can have. You have the opportunity to create a culture in your department; monitor and develop it by means of performance review. There are pitfalls out there, particularly in an anti-managerialist or a-managerialist school, but the transformational effects of placing effective CPD in all its forms at the heart of teacher performance review and teacher motivation will be repaid many times over.

References

Schön, D., *The Reflective Practitioner: How professionals think in action*, London, Temple Smith, 1983.

Hargreaves, A., 'Professional learning communities and performance training sects', in Harris, A. *et al*, *Effective Leadership for School Improvement*, Routledge/Falmer, 2003.

Senge, P. *et al.*, *Schools that Learn*, Nicholas Brearley, 2000.

Rose, Mark, 'Target Practice', *People Management*, 23 November 2000.

Chapter 5

Leading from the middle

Melanie Lincoln

'Large ripples need only small stones.'
(*What's worth fighting for in education?*
A Hargreaves and M Fullan, Open University Press, 1998).

I believe that middle managers like me are the engine-room for innovative and creative thinking in the school environment. We are, after all, the people who have to deliver the overall vision of the leaders of our schools, yet we are also leaders and experts in our own arenas, often more informed about our specific areas of expertise than those who manage us.

I became head of economics and business studies in a GSA school in my third year of teaching. The previous HoD had worked with her two colleagues for the best part of 12 years, very successfully. Subject take-up was healthy and results were excellent. As soon as I arrived I initiated weekly departmental meetings, and tried to maintain constant communication, being highly aware of the accumulated experience around me, and the aura of success.

There is a poem by R D Laing, entitled *Knots*, which encapsulates exactly the situation I found myself in. Not wanting to lose face and respect by appearing too young and too ignorant, but also bursting with ideas and innovation, I found myself in the dangerous situation of maintaining the *status quo* through this ignorance and lack of courage:

> There is something I don't know
> that I am supposed to know.
> I don't know what it is I don't know,
> and yet I am supposed to know.
> And I feel I look stupid

if I seem both not to know it
and not to know what it is I don't know.
Therefore I pretend I know it.
This is nerve-wracking since I don't
know what I must pretend to know.
Therefore I pretend I know everything.

I took advice wherever I could find it, and I initially maintained the *status quo* whilst observing and taking note of everything around me. I absorbed the culture of my new school and formulated my strategy for change in collaboration with my department.

Questions needed answering: Who does my department serve? This obviously included the girls: past, present and future. Beyond the immediate boundaries of the department, whose needs did we serve? Those of fellow staff in collaboration, the girls' parents, senior staff, support staff, the governors and the staff within the department of course. The diverse needs of these groups must form part of the strategic development of the department and their forces must be harnessed for its good; indeed their opinions willingly sought as part of the ongoing strategy for improvement in the department.

The manner by which I achieve continued success within the department depends very much on the style of management I adopt, and the staff's co-operation and understanding of our strategic objectives and how they could be achieved. Michael Fullan has stated that 'Resistance to a new initiative can actually be highly instructive' (*The Jossey-Bass Reader on Educational Leadership*, 2000). Middle management and sixth form staff have to be open to challenge and resistance – the best often invite it and thrive on it. Initially, I felt defensive and rather upset when my ideas were met with resistance. However, what came out of those discussions tended, in retrospect, to be better, and more appropriate to the situation. In the same book, in Chapter 9, Murphy states that:

'While hierarchical strategies for promoting change are becoming outmoded, new strategies that are based on an assumption of mutual dependence need further development. Leaders can achieve results by acting as followers.'

Indeed, by 'following' during my first year, acceptance was gained alongside mutual respect. This may have been incremental change, some may argue: slow and not particularly innovative, certainly not strategic, and definitely not futures thinking – yet it built the foundations for deeper change in the next few years.

Being a new HoD, and perhaps a little idealistic and self-centred, I found it extraordinary that so little research has been carried out on the management of departments specifically, when they play such a vital role in school life. OFSTED and ISI do produce evidence for the performance of departments, yet this is quite dry. Features of effective departments include the importance of pupils, a caring environment, the inclusion of all and so on. 'Ownership' features include the value of a school council, and of whole school strategies regarding behaviour which should be replicated across departments. All this leads towards the clear, shared vision, the engendered climate for change and the expectation of innovation.

I certainly believe that, as teachers within departments, we can get our heads buried in the sand, not see the wood for the trees, be so busy defending our own corner that we do not see what is needed for the greater good. Creating positive politics that empower pupils, parents and colleagues alike requires charm, diplomacy; self-mockery; guilelessness; coming down off one's pedestal, giving voice to others; actively soliciting criticism and dissent; searching for solutions instead of apportioning blame; involving others; encouraging them to lead; asking for their help; lobbying for support; building alliances; listening actively and generally being able to 'lead' what Hargreaves and Fullan call the 'micro-politics of the school' (*op. cit.* 1998).

But who should lead? Those with the acknowledged positions of authority? Or should we all really be trying to fulfil the requirements of positive politics?

In meetings such as those involving heads of departments, often with more than 20 people, open discussion can sometimes be drowned out by the sound of axes being ground. These axes are not in existence just as a result of a general resistance to change; many teachers have discussed the resistance to change in schools exhaustively – indeed, I have done it myself. However I believe these barriers, whether they be fear, resistance to change, poor management in the past, damaged egos, or low self-esteem, can all be overcome with some sense of perspective; of remembering the end goal. We are a caring school; working towards the same goals. Relationships matter.

Teachers, and staff in a school, however, are divided by the very nature of their specialisms into functional departments. Staff are further divided by their pastoral roles, and even further by rank in those roles. Meetings tend to revolve around the routines of school life throughout the year, and the strategy making is saved for those at the very top, usually the senior leadership team (SLT).

Departmental strategy is confined by the school development plan, and school INSET is usually reserved for reactions to recent events and trends such as inspection, and only rarely for proactive research and freedom to work in ways which cut across the usual structures. Teachers speak fondly of creativity in lessons, but we rarely apply it to our work roles and work groups.

One of the greatest constraints, especially at middle management level and at sixth form level, is time. Time can, and of course must, be devoted to planning for change and improving provision for the pupils: this is not in dispute, but teachers, and leaders in teaching, must also remain realistic. Teaching is about the present – how best to serve the present cohort and getting them the best access to the best teaching and learning possible at the time. Yet it is also about planning how to improve it for the future. A balance can and must be sought. As a middle manager operating under the constraints of the examination boards, the school and parents, amongst others, it is increasingly difficult not to become overly prescriptive, if only to finish the syllabus in time for the examination.

The key, as always, is in communication and relationships. If communication with the pupils, with other staff (including the tutor, pastoral leader and SLT) and with parents when necessary, is clear and carefully timed, we can all work together to try to help the pupils succeed, although success or failure is ultimately theirs and they have to take increasing responsibility for their own learning – certainly if we are to prepare them for university and the wider world. If anything, I think we err on the side of over-protecting our pupils, and if we are really to encourage independence in learning, we probably need to be tougher with ourselves sometimes, and allow them to learn through the consequences of some bad decisions and poor choices on their part.

Part of this process is embodied in the theory of *pupil voice*. Professor Jean Ruddock of the University of Cambridge discusses the concept in a paper written for the QCA (*Pupil voice is here to stay!* Address for TTA and DfES conference, 2001), and describes *pupil voice* as 'the consultative wing of pupil participation ... involving discussion about teaching and learning; seeking advice from pupils about new initiatives'.

Pupil voice, however, must again be carried out with strong leadership and a common sense of purpose: it must not be treated as an excuse to whinge about everything that is perceived to be 'wrong' or 'unfair'. It is the careful listening process that goes on; where information is heard, recorded then discussed in other forums. *Pupil voice* seems to work best not so much as a mechanism for decision-making, but more for canvassing opinion.

The school council idea has been implemented in many schools. In our school, each tutor group elects a school council representative who attends meetings on their behalf. The head girl collates ideas for an agenda and chairs the meetings. The empowerment of the students has proved valuable, and indeed the school council embodies the very essence of *pupil voice*, not only giving the students a voice, a channel of communication, but listening to them and making them feel valued.

It is often observed that problems are our friends and that from every difficult situation lessons can be learned, both for the pupils and for staff. I am learning to help them find solutions to their difficulties, and to not take on their problems myself. Sometimes finding a solution whilst having the guidance there, being able to look for solutions and resolution yourself, staff or pupils, can bring further and greater benefits than having someone solve the problem for you.

At the very foundation of any HoD and sixth form teacher's motivation should be the desire to ensure that every pupil under our tutelage leaves full time education equipped not only with the best academic qualifications, but also with the sort of valuable experience and preparation for life beyond school that only a full and varied extra-curricular programme and experienced, motivated staff, can provide.

Life skills learned in the school situation and in the supported wider environment can bring multiple benefits for pupils who leave our care to fulfil their potential in whatever future they choose. The support of parents, staff, and the local community is vital to this end. Communication again plays a vital role here to ensure that pupils can manage the wide variety of experiences on offer.

I believe that the future of any school is to be found in the vision of its current leaders, and that these leaders may not necessarily be those with the formalised positions of management and authority. This is recognised in my current school, and to this end, all staff are encouraged to vocalise their ideas in a spirit of consultative participation. Professional development is encouraged, not just within the academic context but also on a personal level.

Jim Collins in *Good to Great* (Random House, 2001) discusses the need for leaders to get the right people on the bus. He says that in order to have a great organisation, to create an effective community, you do not necessarily need to know at the outset what direction the bus is going in, but that it is crucial to have the right people on that bus – and that they are happy and motivated on their journey.

Modern and all-embracing thinking about planning for the future would suggest that the annual review process of my work, which I carry out every summer, constitutes a somewhat limited and limiting approach to strategic and futures planning. However, within the constraints of the academic year, this is the only time available to complete this process.

I instigated it after my first year (incorporating annotations made to schemes of work throughout the year), and drawing additionally on changes to the school development plan, pupil feedback, INSET and competitive pressures as well as staffing. But it does not have to be incremental and static. It can become dynamic with the flow of time, with weekly meetings through the year building in detailed changes constantly, with out-of-school INSET contributing to broader futures thinking. Isn't the whole point of change to build on the positive and move to the future within the constraints of the present?

Development planning, a major feature of schools these days, has been criticised by analysts such as Davies and Ellison (*The New Strategic*

Direction and Development of the School, Routledge/Falmer, 2003) as bureaucratic, prescriptive and stifling innovation and creativity. I would argue that it depends on the leadership and management of the processes. We have, as middle managers, to jump through these hoops. Why not use them to empower our staff, as a vehicle for creating innovation and creativity?

A characteristic of futures-oriented school leadership is the ability to manage the change process. But middle managers have to do this within the rather prescriptive framework of yearly annual reviews with summer deadlines. As long as middle managers are supported in risk taking, as I was, and have the confidence to move forward into uncharted territories with their staff, the annual processes become the vehicle for change, not the barrier to it.

Having established the futures perspective, a wider view than the next term, or even the next academic year within the confines of the school, thinking more broadly and more ambitiously, it is necessary to establish a departmental strategy that can lead to action and change. It is clear here, that merely having a futures perspective can be enough. No-one can accurately predict the future, but to be merely aware of its possibilities, to be flexible enough to cope with what the future may bring, and not to be as surprised by the future as the next person, can be sufficient.

Finally, the engine room needs oil and a service on occasion: passionate teachers need interaction with, and support from, others to avoid becoming exhausted. Believing in the school, having loyalty to the message, joining in, even in the smallest of ways, forging relationships, building trust and reciprocity, all this is evident at our school, led from the front by our SLT, and this is the equivalent of a damn good service.

Other recommended reading:
Field, J. *Social Capital*, Routledge, 2003.
Fullan, M. *Change Forces – Probing the Depths of Educational Reform.* London: Falmer Press, 1993.
Hamel, G. and Prahalad, C.K. *Strategic Intent.* Harvard Business Review 67, (3), 1989.
Harris, A., Bennett, N. and Preedy, M. *Organisational effectiveness*

and improvement in education, esp. ch. 19 by Fullan, M. The Open University Press, 1998.

Hazler, R. J. *Helping in the Hallways.* Thousand Oaks, California: Corwin Press, 1998.

National College for School Leadership. *What Leaders Read* 1. (2003).

Rittenhaus, L.J. *Leadership and the Inner Journey* – Parker Palmer interview (Leader to Leader, Fall 2001).

We are grateful to Taylor and Francis Books (UK) for permission to quote from *Knots*: Selected works by R.D. Laing, (1970).

Chapter 6

The limits of autonomy: curriculum and qualifications

Andrew Grant

Back in a long-ago golden age of school mastering, before either the National Curriculum or league tables were visited upon an unsuspecting education system; when, in short, I began my teaching career, my head of department kept all that was needful for the administration of one of the school's largest departments in his sock drawer. This reposed in his bedroom on a grim corridor for bachelor staff known universally, and with no appreciable irony, as *Death Row*.

Even in that un-bureaucratic period, this was acknowledged to be a somewhat extreme homage to the cult of the gentleman amateur, but it was sufficient unto the day. The department did in fact possess a filing cabinet, just one, located in a windowless seminar room, but its contents had scarcely changed in three decades. It consisted solely of past examination papers, all from the same board, to which one new set was added each summer.

It didn't really matter. The proportion of the national cohort doing A levels was small; the number achieving A grades was tiny and the relationship between grades and either intelligence or admission to a good university quite indiscernible. So it was that when, after a succession of frustrating results at O level, the head of department tentatively suggested changing exam boards, he called down on his head (and *from* his Head) a denunciation of truly pharisaical pomposity at this unprincipled prostitution of his department in grubby pursuit of mere results.

For you, dear reader, a newly-appointed, ambitious, aspirational, energetic and imaginative 21st century HoD, the case could hardly be more altered. You are confronted with infinite riches in a little room: a bewildering wealth of curricular choice beyond the dreams of your predecessors. But how much freedom to bring to fruition your vision of your department do you enjoy in reality? Are you bounded in a nutshell or do you count yourself a king of infinite space? And no prizes for guessing of which department I was once head.

To begin with the case above. Heads now have an ambivalent relationship with league tables. We all agree to regard them with Olympian disdain, but would much prefer to do so from an Olympian height in those very same tables, since there can then, of course, be no suspicion of sour grapes in our contempt.

A mere change of awarding body is unlikely to be contentious – if you want to change, it is likely to be in anticipation of better results – but bear in mind that each suite of examinations has its own characteristics and foibles. Even if the syllabus is one with which you are personally familiar, a department with long experience of one board will have a genuine learning curve to travel. There can be no guarantee of an instant upturn in results and there may even be a dip in the first year, which you will have to justify.

Prepare your arguments well, above all, in terms of the appropriateness of the new syllabus and its educational benefits to your particular students, because the change will inevitably bring costs – in time spent attending training sessions and familiarisation with the new syllabuses – and possibly financial, should it involve investment in a whole new set of course books and/or materials or if the new awarding body is not one for which your school is already an accredited centre. Beware, too, of opportunity costs in jettisoning the experience of any members of your department who may be examiners for the existing syllabus.

If the proposed change is to an entirely different qualification, all of the above will apply, but you are now potentially raising an issue of whole-school strategy and you are likely to have to make a still stronger case to your immediate colleagues, to senior management and perhaps to pupils and to parents.

From your point of view as a HoD, it is entirely proper for your judgement to be led by what will offer your pupils the best educational experience in your subject. However, all schools operate in a market context; the market is both internal and external and the ripples from almost anything your department does will rock other boats.

It is not part of the direct purpose of this chapter to discuss the relative merits of different qualifications; that is a matter for a HoD to decide. My principal aim is merely to suggest the constraining factors you might need to take into account in proposing a given course of action, so that, if necessary, you have your counter-arguments ready when the inevitable objections are raised.

It is, I suppose, axiomatic by definition that no single department can go it alone in teaching towards a grouped diploma qualification. These currently appear in a variety of guises. However, some, like the AQA and the Pre-U diplomas, it would not be too much of a caricature to describe as shiny wrappers for free-standing qualifications, with the important and valuable additional requirement of a substantial extended project or piece of independent research – and in these it might be possible for an individual department to give a lead unilaterally.

Certainly, you might make a name for yourself within the school by trialling, say, AQA's free-standing Level 3 extended project in your own subject area, and if this qualified some of your students for the diploma, so much the better. Organisation and monitoring will be the biggest challenge and your chief consideration will need to be to find an acceptably fallow time in the sixth form calendar when students can focus on it without it interfering with the rest of their work in your subject or in others. The post-AS exam period comes to mind. Ultimately, when other departments begin to get in on the act, it will need discussion and decisions at a whole-school level, if an assessed extended project is to be fully embedded in the school's sixth form provision.

The government's own diplomas, which appear, at the time of writing, to be much more in the nature of a genuine grouped award from which the individual elements cannot be unpacked, are as yet an untested, if not totally unknown, quantity. What is known suggests that the organisational demands will be very considerable indeed – considerable enough to demand that schools work in consortia, not only to cover between them the full range of subjects, but to manage the work experience requirement.

The obvious choice for a tried and tested high quality grouped award is of course, therefore, the International Baccalaureate Diploma (IB). If you, as a head of department, feel strongly, perhaps from successful previous experience, that that is the direction in which the school should be travelling, it will be up to you to advance the cause through the school's political channels, formal and informal, and, unless you are preaching to an already half-converted senior management who need only a last push, you must face the fact that it may be a long job if you are starting from scratch.

If you are new to the school, you will need to assess the kinds of students and the kind of school you are now dealing with, to satisfy yourself that what worked in your last place will work equally well here. Much of the interest in the IB derives from its proven ability to differentiate more finely than A level at the higher end of the ability range but those with practical experience of teaching it are confident that it is accessible to those with more modest intellectual equipment, too.

Equally, most A level teachers will be aware of students who have appeared quite middling at GCSE, but who have turned into absolute stars at A level, when allowed to specialise, and when liberated from the need to study subjects they simply can't get on with. It's your call; you must know your pupils.

The IB is an impressive and well-respected qualification and its advocates are persuasive. In opting for it, a school is buying into a whole curricular philosophy. As a whole-curriculum offer, it makes considerable demands on curricular time and will bring with it substantial costs in training and increased staffing. A day school, run on a lean budget and using its time intensively before the buses leave in the evening, may find those demands and costs more difficult to meet than a boarding school, and it could struggle to accommodate the IB's curricular demands without either sacrificing highly-valued extra-curricular activities or incorporating into the diploma what has traditionally been voluntary.

Running A level in parallel alongside the IB will bring its own special challenges. The smaller the school, perhaps the greater the challenge, in that twin-tracking will be impossible if there is only one set per subject, whilst co-teaching two qualifications simultaneously to A level students and IB students in the same set will, to say the least, pose organisational challenges. That can be, and is, done successfully, but, it appears, generally with fearsomely bright pupils who are naturally independent learners. The mismatch of examination timings between the two systems, even if the A level approach is entirely linear, could also play havoc with the coherence of the teaching programme at crucial times of the year.

Deliberations on matters such as these, even if they originate in the large forum of a HoDs meeting, are likely to be taken forward, for practical reasons, by a much smaller body, designated 'curriculum steering group' or something similar, chaired by the academic deputy or director of studies.

Within such a group, some departments, particularly those that are *de jure* or *de facto* 'faculties': science, languages; maths; English; are likely to have a status akin to that of permanent members of the UN Security Council. If you're not among them, you might do well to forge some alliances with the aim of securing a voice at the table speaking for other subject groupings with interests in common: creative, social sciences, humanities, *etc.*

The Head and senior management, meanwhile, will be making a judgement on how well such a move would be received by pupils already at the school and their parents and those of prospective pupils. That judgement will involve intimate knowledge of the catchment area, of the sophistication of the market and of what local competitors are doing. A change of this scale will involve governors, too, because it is central to the school's identity and its unique selling point.

Moving to an alternative free-standing qualification, such as the IGCSE or the Pre-U, will involve far less structural upheaval, because in each case they are designed to be taught on a similar allocation of directed time to existing mainstream qualifications. Nevertheless, a number of the considerations above will still be very pertinent.

The advent of universal modularity at GCSE, might, I predict, accelerate the trend towards IGCSE and in most subjects I would anticipate you meeting little serious objection. Heads and directors of studies may be less than enthusiastic about extending downwards by two years the disruption to teaching familiar from successive modular A level examination sessions, but parental opinion may equate maximising their offspring's chances of the highest possible grades with offering them the greatest possible number of opportunities to score marks.

A neat way of neutralising that pressure might be to teach a course whose assessment can only be linear. However, if your subject is English, or maths, or a science, or a modern language – in short one of the qualifying subjects required to reach the 5A*-C threshold for the enhanced DCSF GCSE performance tables, and for which IGCSEs are not currently recognised – you may find that the choice becomes a strategic, whole-school one about which the Head will have a strong view. Up to now the government has refused to include IGCSE results in its annual performance tables, so schools undertaking them in qualifying subjects score 'nil'.

A super-selective, oversubscribed academic school hunting at the top of the food chain among the local competition, with a sophisticated and knowledgeable clientele and a reputation so established as to be bomb-proof, might well enjoy and benefit from the *chutzpah* of a position at the bottom of the LEA table.

Not so an undersubscribed school in a less affluent and demographically declining region, selective only in theory and struggling to compete with a good comprehensive and a sixth form college in the same town, a new Academy in the next city and a grammar school across the county boundary. For them, a high place in the LEA performance table in January's national dailies may be a crucial feature of the annual marketing programme.

The IB and the IGCSE are, of course, established qualifications that enjoy a well-proven welcome at the most prestigious universities. Though it has yet to be put to the test, all the indications are that universities will also smile benevolently on the Pre-U; indeed, QCA has bestowed its blessing upon CIE's new infant. As has been well trailed, it is intended to be mix-and-match-able with A level and designed to provide more differentiation among the ablest candidates; to provide a linear, more traditionally-assessed course, of greater volume than A level, with opportunities for more open-ended, discursive responses, offering a better preparation for the first year of university than an A level course assessed in tightly-directed bite-sized chunks and in which 25% of candidates nationally achieve the highest possible grade. What's not to like about that then?

Assuming the revisions to A level and the advent of the A* have not shot their fox anyway, the lingering concern about pre-U is how accessible it will be to the hewers of wood and drawers of water who would probably be a safe-ish bet for a C grade at A level. To be fair, CIE have been at great pains to reassure everyone on this score.

Accepting their assurances at face value, a head of department attracted to the Pre-U will therefore want to assess the likely effect on subject recruitment of a product that might reward with a grade 3 a candidate who would be a certain grade A prospect at A level, and indeed goes on to get exactly that in his/her other three (A level) subjects. Senior management, meanwhile, will be focusing on the external market, in attempting to second-guess how parents will react to results that don't lend themselves quite so readily to dinner-party bragging rights. ("Yes, Tarquin got straight threes. We're so proud!")

What you are unlikely to have access to, as yet, in all of the above examples, are management and monitoring tools such as MidYIS and ALIS, developed for mainstream qualifications by the CEM Centre, charting value-added against baseline tests taken by a sample large enough to provide some assurance of validity. The strategic use of these was dealt with in an earlier chapter. It will be necessary, over time, for you to gather data to develop your own target-setting and monitoring techniques, but for the first couple of years you and your colleagues will be flying blind.

Beware then, of initiative overload. Getting your mind round a new qualification, internalising it and becoming confident in teaching it, takes time, effort and a good deal of emotional energy and you do get better with practice. It would be asking a great deal of your department to take on more than one major curricular change at one time.

Let us suppose, though, that you suppress your revolutionary zeal and decide to play the conventional hand you've been dealt, at least for a year or two. What freedom of manoeuvre do you have as a head of department; what are the opportunities, what the pitfalls; how do you avoid shooting yourself in the foot; how do you win the approval or opprobrium of your colleagues?

As already suggested, the increased number of assessment opportunities that modular examinations bring with them has made serious inroads into teaching time. If your school has a policy of, for example, forbidding January entries in the lower sixth, you will have to abide by it, or present a very persuasive case for exemption. In my experience it seems that only mathematicians really cannot live without regular fixes of examination modules.

But it is not only external examinations that disrupt teaching in this way. If, because it suits the sequence in which you approach the syllabus, you unilaterally decide to hold mock examinations for your subject at an unconventional time, even if you confine them to lessons for which your subject is already timetabled, the distraction they cause to pupils who temporarily lose focus on their other subjects will not make you popular.

In this regard, the annual collision of coursework deadlines is a major culprit, and outbreaks of strategic illness, overt cutting of lessons and general goings-AWOL are not unheard of (a splendid example of litotes: deliberate understatement to make a point) at such seasons, as students try to compensate at the last minute for an utter inability to plan ahead and/or prioritise.

This is a vice that once appeared to afflict boys more than girls, but the advent of the mobile phone and the social networking site, relieving young people of the need ever to engage in any kind of forward planning, even socially, appears to have brought about some gender-correction and girls are catching up (or regressing). I suspect the move to controlled-conditions assessment of coursework that will come in with the revised GCSE syllabuses will merely swap old kinds of coursework pressures for new ones with no net reduction in the distraction factor.

A well-organised school will publish a timetable of coursework deadlines and a policy on how late submissions will be dealt with. It really is in all departments' interests to abide by it. If the policy is a particularly draconian one, ruling that submissions after the school's internal deadline will not be considered even though the exam board's deadline has not yet passed, you may be tempted towards leniency, in the interests of your department's overall results. Don't. You will be undermining your colleagues and will come to regret it yourself when your reputation as a soft touch comes to haunt you.

Other opportunities for irritating your fellow heads of department include boosting recruitment to your subject by subverting the school's reporting and grading policy in Year 9 through inflating the number of A/A* grades you award in your subject for the reports that are issued just before pupils make their GCSE option choices. That could, in any case, rebound on you in the results two years later.

In general, in fact, you are likely to find that any direct hyping of your subject, covert or overt, that is not part of a balanced whole-school presentation of options, will be viewed as, at the very least, un-gentlemanly, if not deviously Machiavellian. Arranging a Year 11 field trip or an out-of-school revision lecture in mid-May is another excellent way to attract the venom of your fellow HoDs, who really will not appreciate the decimation of their sets just at the time when they are racing to complete, at worst, the syllabus, at best, their carefully-structured revision programme.

Entering pupils early for GCSE in your subject, in Year 10, or even Year 9, may seem an attractive way of enhancing the profile of the department and stretching the brightest. So it can be, but it needs careful planning in a whole-school context. Some high-achieving prep schools make it a point of honour to bring their pupils up to the threshold of GCSE standard, in Latin and French for example, before Common Entrance and they do so very effectively, presenting the receiving school with a dilemma.

Obviously you can't have such able pupils marking time for two years and the obvious answer is to let them knock off GCSE at the end of Year 10 or even Year 9. This can have the added whole-school benefit of taking some of the pressure off in Year 11, leading to more time for other subjects and better results all round, but see the caveat below.

Especially if you are contemplating a Year 9 entry, what you must have, if you don't want to cut off your supply of the ablest candidates in your subject before they even think about A level, is a coherent and challenging post-GCSE programme that isn't going to be relegated too much to the back burner in Years 10 and 11 in competition with the pressing demands of all the other GCSEs.

Otherwise, they are likely to take the opportunity simply to cast the net wider in their GCSE choices and leave your subject behind for ever. For classicists, a possibility might be to offer ancient Greek GCSE, but an obvious answer for any subject is to begin an AS course, albeit on half the normal time allocation, with the implicit expectation that, having got so far towards AS level by the end of Year 11, the pupils will want to complete the job, with the promise of outstanding A level grades in prospect.

All of this, of course, is predicated on the school's policy on setting by ability making it a possibility for your subject. Similar strictures apply in mirror image if the norm is for GCSE to be taken early, but you have a group of pupils for whom acceleration is not desirable and/or to whom you need to offer learning support. If the setting policy doesn't allow it, again, you will need to work through the curriculum steering group to get things moved in the direction you want.

In either case, given the emphasis that university admissions tutors place on candidates' GCSE profiles, you will need to be able to answer any challenge from parents or senior management that you are risking top grades for the sake of early ones. The best way to do that, of course, is to accelerate only candidates for whom an A* is a realistic expectation at the time they take the exam.

If all of your strategies are succeeding, and your department is riding the crest of a wave, you may be tempted to branch out by offering a new, but related, subject: politics as well as history; philosophy as well as religious studies; business studies as well as economics, drama as well as English; ancient history as well as Latin. Fine, good, good luck, but beware hubris.

Your Head may not react well if you are asking for the recruitment of extra staff because, instead of the usual three nice, cost-effective, A level sets of 12 in history, you suddenly have three history sets of nine and two politics sets of eight, whilst the classics department finds itself overstaffed because you have appropriated a set's worth of potential Latinists. You'll be even less popular the following year, when the additional 16 periods becomes 32 as you acquire both AS and A2 sets, while another department is facing redundancies because the head of economics has insisted on her right to follow the precedent you have set, and business studies is making a killing at the expense of geography. It could all come back to bite you when, the following year, the religious studies department, in self defence, starts offering philosophy, which proves far more popular among Year 11's most gifted intellectual poseurs than history, to which you were anticipating recruiting them.

Other ways in which you might seek to maximise the attractiveness and performance of your department include offering extension classes and extended project provision or 'twilight' revision clinics after school. These sorts of initiatives are likely to find favour in principle with pupils, parents and senior management, but, as ever, be aware of whose boat you may be rocking.

I well remember the overwhelming indignation I felt on being instructed by the director of studies to discontinue the S level classes I had set up in a free period of mine that happened to coincide with study periods for the relevant members of my A level set. His reasoning was that the period in question, though not specifically timetabled for teaching, was technically allocated to be available as the ninth period (beyond the eight taught ones) to another subject.

I was furious at the time, seeing it as a repression of intellectual endeavour, a frustration of initiative, a spurning of my voluntary offering of time in pursuit of excellence and many other high-minded and self-righteous perceived injuries. Now, I see his point. Precedents are dangerous things, especially when, if they were universally followed, the system would collapse, and these days I hear myself saying, in similar circumstances, much the same thing as my former oppressor.

Likewise, after-school classes are admirable and show the kind of selfless commitment that makes our schools what they are. However, you can't make them compulsory (except as a sanction for a particular shortcoming) and you can't rely on them to complete the syllabus. You should not expect attendance at your *ad hoc* classes, however admirable, to trump choir practice or rugby training if one or the other is an established priority on that evening and there will always be pupils who, for entirely legitimate reasons, will not be able to make a particular after-school session. To deny them teaching crucial to the course would be inequitable.

However, a flourishing subject-specific society with a programme of meetings, visits and lectures by eminent speakers, is a great way to popularise your subject and to capture the enthusiasm of the ablest with the sense that what is going on in your department is a central and exciting part of the school's intellectual life.

By now, you may be tempted to conclude that, for a head of department, the path through the minefield would be perfectly safe if it were not for the elephant traps, trip wires and predatory wildlife, but you would be wrong.

To be a HoD is one of the most exciting jobs in a school. You have a wonderful opportunity to share the passion for your subject, which presumably brought you into teaching in the first place, with intelligent young people beyond those sitting in your own lessons.

You have a chance to make your subject important in their lives now and in the future and perhaps to communicate a love for it that they will pass on to their own children to make that future a better one. You will set the agenda for, with luck, like-minded colleagues, who share that passion. Your job is sufficiently hands-on and your decisions sufficiently significant for the feedback to be immediate and direct.

A school resembles the mediaeval metaphor of the body politic. The parts cannot live independently of the whole, but equally, the health of the whole relies on the fitness of the parts. You have charge, as it were, of a vital organ. You will have to learn to live with accountability, but, even if you go on to climb higher on the greasy pole of leadership, rarely again will you experience to quite such a degree the direct, un-delegated connection between the choices you make and the outcomes they bring; between your pupils' success and your responsibility for it.

Chapter 7

The HoD's role in teacher recruitment and retention

John Newton

'In conclusion, Miss Dove is a superb teacher and I shall be sorry to lose her.' It is the clinching statement in any reference. If you read it, it tells you to snap her up. If you have just written it, someone else is going to do the snapping.

A competent and conscientious HoD wishes to recruit and retain the best people, because bad people are a nightmare. They will take up an inordinate amount of your time on unfruitful tasks, whether through poor relations in the department, complaints from parents or a lack of will to seize your vision and move forward with you. Get this wrong, and the outlook is not rosy.

So Miss Dove sidles up to you and tells you she is moving on. She is a quality young teacher and has done three good years. She has gained a position as a head of department. You knew it was in the air, but now it is confirmed. Rejoice. You have done something good for a fellow professional.

Think strategically: what does Miss Dove's departure mean? Change is opportunity. Before looking for Miss Dove Mark ll, stand back and ponder where the department is and where it is going: new courses; changes in direction in the school at large; the make-up of the department. What skills are missing? What new challenges lie ahead? Reflect on where you wish to be in three years' time. Miss Dove Mark ll may be precisely what you are NOT looking for, even though Miss Dove Mark l was a triumph.

While you are deep into such worthy thoughts, your Head is holding the letter of resignation and has other thoughts. The pressure on schools to control staffing budgets, the other roles that Miss Dove fulfilled beyond the classroom and the need always to have staff who promote the school mean that the Head's agenda may be very different from yours.

And then there is the matter of timing. Just as asparagus is best picked in spring and you should never harvest oysters in a month spelt with an 'r', so there is a propitious time to recruit good staff. It is the first two terms of the academic year. Sometimes that moment is out of your control, and if you see Easter hurtling towards you, get moving. The summer is not a good time for finding new and high-quality teachers.

Therefore do your best to control the debate. Talk to the Head, talk to the director of studies and, crucially, talk to your department. Your colleagues will provide a rich tapestry of views, including some that had not occurred to you. Finally, look at yourself. Are you carrying the IT burden when someone else could do it, allowing you to focus on the new exam specification? Is it time for a new person to take on the organisation of the department society or to write the Year 9 scheme of work, leaving you to focus more on A level? I repeat: change is opportunity.

This is a marketplace: sell yourself. Wonderful as your school may be, with yet another set of record-breaking results last summer, do not assume that good staff are automatically low hanging on the tree waiting to be plucked. Some will have read stories that many independent schools are not paying salaries at market rate. Even if most HMC and GSA schools offer competitive salaries, the teaching unions are now banging on about how much harder life is in smaller independent schools; Charles Dickens would have a field day, and we can sometimes be tainted by association. To ensure that the net is cast as wide as possible, you must promote yourself.

The *TES* is the obvious place to advertise, but these days there are many online recruitment sites. There are also many fine teacher training institutions bursting with bright young things (if that is what you want). Consider how you will access the best people and make sure that the advert has impact. You should work on this with the Head and director of studies.

Is the application pack the first experience of the expectations of you and the school that the prospective member of staff will have? Perhaps. Perhaps not. More likely it is your section of the website. Good candidates are savvy. They are looking for more than just good pay. They are not desperate to come to you. They want a department with the professional appeal and the sense of direction that will launch them into the next stage of their careers. How good is your micro-site? Are the pictures unflattering? The results out of date? Is there buzz and fizz? Expect them to surf your way, and make sure that they will like what they read there.

All the same, the pack sent to the candidates is an essential element in the process. Do you know what goes out? Is the Head's office still using an old job description that refers to the banda machine? If you sow dullness and lack of creativity, so you will reap.

Then there is the personal dimension. Do the job details make the region sound attractive, with practical details about house buying, local amenities *etc*? They may revere your school, but shouldn't you warn them about the less salubrious areas nearby? This is unashamedly a selling exercise and how you, the school, the Head and the department come across is vital.

The application pack is also the first step in the successful candidate's induction. Many leaders are clear on the values of their team, but fail to promote them effectively. Then they wonder why they are not understood or implemented or shared. The minute a candidate picks up the pack of information you send out, or clicks on your microsite, (s)he is imbibing what your department and your school is all about. You are stating your expectations and shaping theirs: the virtuous cycle has begun.

Shark infested waters? The sharks are the lawyers who earn their bread from bad employers who discriminate or mistreat applicants for jobs. This aspect of the recruitment process has changed beyond recognition in the last ten years. Anti-discrimination legislation, as well as safer recruitment processes, have had a deep impact on how we conduct ourselves. Safe recruitment is more for your Head to worry about, but the potential minefield you are entering as someone with direct involvement with interviewing and selecting candidates needs some thought.

To prevent us slipping helplessly into a mire of legalese, I would suggest you ensure that you are properly trained on what you can, and cannot, say in interview. Questions such as "How long before you get pregnant, Mrs

Smith?" are not only risible: they are actionable, and you would do well to have yourself and your fellow HoDs trained up on the niceties.

The same applies to the selection process. Every school does this differently. Some collect the CVs and application forms in a central place for scrutiny by anyone who might have an interest in the eventual decision. Some restrict them to just a few lucky sets of eyes belonging to those who do the shortlist before putting the CVs on more general release. Some copy applications, but keep the references firmly in the Head's office, and some Heads show them to everyone else involved in the interviews only *after* the candidates have been put through their paces.

It appears to me, as a Head, that CVs and application forms are getting longer and longer, and the more experienced eyes on the matter the better. But beware no-one scribbles 'too old' in big letters across their papers. Remember the sharks. Remember too that professional confidentiality is important: unsuccessful candidates will not thank you if everyone back at their present school hears that they applied.

I am especially keen on application forms. They standardise the information and ask perhaps awkward questions that a CV can hide. You may wish to have some input at the planning stage on what should go into such a form so that the true colours of the candidates stand out. Indeed if your school has not reviewed its selection processes of late (and most schools have done so, in the wake of safe recruitment requirements), it would be well worth urging that it be done. Remember that it becomes much harder to change it once the juggernaut of the academic year has begun to roll.

When reading the CVs we return to strategy. What are the skills and qualities that you would ideally want? This is the starting point for an effective reading of a CV and application form. Get ahead here. Unless the Head is qualified in your subject, (s)he could be wooed by the proclamations of professional zeal that seem to be the staple of the modern covering letter.

'I am particularly impassioned by the writings of the 17th century Russians, especially Tolstoy, whose poetic command of his native tongue resonates with the deepest recesses of all the souls of my pupils.' Your Head is a chemist. *You* are the Russianist. Tolstoy was 19th century and wrote novels. You have to help the hapless HM from buying this junk. Assert yourself if you need to.

So you have hacked through the verbiage of the front three pages of close type and have formed something of an opinion on the candidate's academic motivation and interests. Beware, it may still be guff. You need next to dig into the CV and find the qualifications. These will say whether there is substance behind the claims. Here it is easy to dismiss someone who has a degree from somewhere you are unfamiliar with. Don't leap to conclusions.

Universities, like schools, can be very good, even nationally renowned, for a given subject. Warwick, for example, has gained a remarkable reputation for business studies and maths. Cardiff is now turning out great scientists. I can attest to the quality of the law course at Exeter. One could go on. You don't want to overlook a star, because the course is not immediately familiar.

Going back even further (call me old fashioned), I still lay a lot of store on a candidate who has a top grade at A level in your subject. Do you want your Oxbridge class to get wind of the fact that the person teaching them did not score an A at A level? Morale would founder – unless they can convince you that their late development is genuine. You should also be alive to the possibility that the best teacher is not necessarily the best qualified person in the field.

A decent CV will list, briefly, the wider professional duties the candidate has undertaken. These can be telling. If the candidate has been appointed to be master i/c Post-it notes, you should smell a rat. If they have been given the ICT brief in the department, that is of more interest. If they have run the subject's society and can list some achievements, you may have found yourself someone who is trusted in their present department to take on more and who could bring an extra dimension to yours.

What about newly qualified or about-to-qualify candidates? I have developed quite a faith in PGCE courses of late. It is becoming increasingly hard to make a success of the profession without formal preparation, although there is still the odd gem out there who is a natural (some even become Headmasters and write in learned books...). The best PGCE candidates will have had the chance to do some extra work or prove their mettle in some way. Schools which offer teaching practice do not tend to exploit their PGCE students unless they are good value. It creates more work than a host school wishes to bear if it goes wrong.

So take their various short term exploits in their teaching practice seriously. But whatever their competence, a surfeit of newly-qualified teachers can place quite a burden on your deputy in charge of induction – and on you. The process of gaining qualified teacher status is labyrinthine and you only want to be steering a certain number of candidates through it at any one time.

A personal point of interest is just the right touch of the humorous or personal, something that gives away the candidate's character. What you are looking for is more than just a classroom practitioner and someone to sit opposite you in a departmental meeting. You might find yourself running the annual excursion to Greece or the field trip to the Outer Hebrides with this person.

Can you sit in a plane with them for three hours? Do you think they would be hopeless with pupils outside the formal school context? There is something about the 'face that fits'. The chemistry with you and the department is vital if they can support the tougher or less conventional activities that are part of your department's calling.

By now you should have picked up the formal and informal, the personal and professional, and in some cases the sacred and profane aspects to the candidates. You will then need to go into combat with the director of studies and the Head to secure the shortlist you want. Be in negotiating mode to some extent, but it is vital to remember that you are the one who will have to line manage this person and not the Head in the first instance. Your view is important. At the end of the process you should have a list of manageable length, containing names of those who you think can do the job.

Ensure that you do not invite too many. You have a lot to pack in. Yes, by all means have a ranked reserve list, but take three, or four, or even five if you can stretch to two days, but after four (certainly, in a single day), I suggest that your heads will be swimming.

The big day comes. I know of schools that still get this so wrong. I repeat, you are selling as well as buying in this process, so be aware of how the day is designed. You may not have the overall say, but ultimately you do not wish a very good fish to get away because the programme was not fully and properly planned. Indeed write out a proper programme for them and for you and email it to them before they come ... and don't forget to include the school tour.

All candidates should be asked to teach a lesson. Provide details as early as you can about it and the pupils who will be receiving it. Explain issues about expenses and accommodation. You don't want a good candidate to pick up that you are not on top of the essentials and courtesies. I hope that your department is a biddable enough bunch for you to be proud to present the candidates to them. In many, many cases, your colleagues will be a major selling point for the subject and the school. Lunch with the candidates is a winner. They feel welcomed and you have a chance for another insight into their characters.

If your school does not have a culture of 'meet and greet', you may lose that desirable applicant and end up with an also-ran. Do members of staff from other departments introduce themselves when the applicant is sitting in the common room or reception? Risky, I know, but what about the issue of whether the candidates meet the pupils – perhaps for a tour of the school?

You will choose the lesson they teach with care so that they do not have unequal tasks – one teaching the total angels in the third form and another with the class from Hades in the fifth. As a courtesy, check with the candidate that (s)he feels that the nature of the lesson and the behaviour of the pupils gave them a fair chance to show what they are made of. If the ICT gave out (unheard of, I know), be understanding.

For the lesson, some schools prefer to have two staff to observe – yourself as HoD and a seasoned pro, possibly an inspector – someone who is involved in every recruitment process. They will know what sort of teacher fits – or does not. Your director of studies may well be the right person for this. The pupils will enjoy the trust you show in them if you are open to feedback. However, I would not invite it as it will suddenly need to become part of the official criteria and a candidate may cry foul. All the same, our pupils are unerring in their judgements. If they give the thumbs down, proceed with caution.

The interview itself: many years ago, a colleague of mine was invited down to a coastal boarding school for interview and spent the evening before in the sea with the Headmaster and his family. Interviewing has become a little more formal than it used to be. What are the key elements?

The cold dead hand of the law no longer condones the wide-ranging conversation that HoDs used to enjoy. In order to protect the school from accusations of unfairness or discrimination, you have to adopt a systematic approach to questions in all interviews, although asking the same question in two different interviews in the day might be most revealing. However, once you get beneath those formal 'starter' questions, you have some leeway to begin to probe responses with more individual questions. If you can, try to get to know each candidate over a chat at break or lunch. Social chat at the interview itself may mean you overrun, and that is unhelpful for all.

The best advice about interviews is never to offer the question to which a glib "yes" or "no" is required. Ask for descriptions and examples. Provide case studies and "what if..?" scenarios. You will get more out of your candidate that way. You must give them a chance to shine. Sometimes a candidate will take a very open-ended and apparently innocuous question off into some lengthy and very revealing responses: "Looking back, how do you feel about your A level results?" can be one of these.

Take notes by all means, but as ever remember not to write something that may one day end up on a file as evidence of bias. Accusations of ageism, sexism, homophobia – there is no fury like a candidate scorned. It is also therefore worthwhile having a standard mark grid for all interviewers so that you can justify your choice even if the reasons are more qualitative than quantitative. Some Heads even go as far as to advise that you should never interview anyone on your own as you lay yourself open to the 'your word against mine' situation that is never happily resolved. In the current climate, I believe that is going too far, but the day may come...

Decision time. Each school does this differently. However, I have one very strong word of advice. No Head worth their salt is going to appoint someone whom *you* do not want. Therefore, know what you want before you go in. Your steer is the most important. There may be diverse views in the room; there may be reflections from many parties; but the quality of the lesson and the potential rapport with you and the department should be the ultimately determining factors.

And once your mind is made up, the Head will expect you to stick with it. Nothing annoys a Head so much as when a teacher turns out to be a bad appointment and the HoD begins to mutter around the common room that (s)he didn't want them in the first place.

There is a wrinkle here. The references may have only gone to a select group. You may not be aware of crucial factors in the application and may therefore have been sold a pup. This is more a question for the Head than you, but you have a right to ask who has access to the CVs. It may make the process cleaner, and the decision one that can be owned by all.

Retention starts now. Once the decision is made, the call put through and the candidate secured, it does not end there. Retention starts immediately. First impressions count for so much in this business. Their impression of you as an interviewer is now put to the back of the mind. Their impression of you as colleague and line manager now begins.

I make a habit of sending an email to my senior staff and the relevant HoD as soon as I have a decision from a candidate. This enables staff to begin to make contact and build up an acquaintance. You should also have your own induction process in mind: one that marries well with the general scheme for all new staff. It is reassuring to work with a HoD who gets on the personal and professional front foot early.

It is the dream in this business to have a settled team that ticks over with gifted, likable staff who provide a first class service and give the HoD a quiet and successful life. To achieve that, the staff you choose must always believe that you have their best interests at heart. At some point, they will need to be assured that you care about their personal circumstances as much as you do about their effectiveness as a professional. Much as we hope these factors will not break into school life, it is likely that at some point they will.

It is said of Sir Alex Ferguson that he knows something about everyone in his club; that he can wander the corridors of Manchester United, past the fans sipping chardonnay (and the players with wives so named), to the cleaners and ground staff, and have a personal conversation.

We are moving away from those very male top-down norms of leadership that involve insensitive talking, messages from on high, pulling rank and institutional fagging. Female leaders have taught us a very good and very different way. Care for the whole person and they will do well at the job you want them to do. Not only that, but they will enjoy it too!

So, warmly welcome your new member of staff – not at the start of the next academic year, but in one, two or three visits in advance. Solder the rapport between them and the department. Ensure they get to know the common room before they arrive and give them that buzz, that sense of anticipation that will mean a flying and happy start. Let them see some summer term lessons, especially if it's their first job. Pay travel expenses. It is part of their training – a subject for a subsequent chapter, but it starts here.

In my career, I always looked for Heads and HoDs whom I thought would support my aspirations and know me personally. I am privileged to hold a collection of very positive memories of all the persons I have worked for and I believe that they were instrumental in getting the most out of me. That is not to suggest that you should speak about career progression from the word go, but you should be aware of your newly acquired teacher's aspirations and give them the time and space to begin to reveal them to you. It may be that they have no clear pathway before them. Many do not. This will be a happy experience if a new and purposeful member of staff gives you their best, knowing that you will support any future move.

Be alive to the fact that good professionals, like you, want more out of their job than money. They want to see their pupils win high honours and they want to feel part of a team that is taking the subject and the school to a higher place. They want to feel that they belong, and that they have been part of the success.

They also want to hear from you where they must gain more experience in order to be ready for the next move. Truly great staff will have that instinct for self-criticism already and act upon it. This could help you as they might take on a bigger brief in the department. However you may also find that they want more experience of extra-curricular activities or boarding, in which case you have to be willing to let them grow and change outside the confines of your departmental domain too. There is nothing worse than a 'me in my small corner' HoD. Staff become resentful and the school is poorer for it.

One could go much further into the subtleties and nuances of human management at this point. There is a considerable body of literature on it already. One thing worth noting is that those departments that eat together work well together. Where you can turn the chores into a pleasure – the field trip, the odd departmental meeting, the exchange (why go to France when you can go to Canada or Senegal?) – do so. And be reconciled to the fact that good people move on. It does not mean that you have done a bad job or that the school is deficient. It just shows that you chose the right person.

Of course, you may soon discover to your horror that they were the wrong decision. First of all, don't panic. There are ways and means out of such a situation. Make sure you consult with your superiors, remain fair, remain impartial, keep confidences and keep notes on everything. But let us not dwell on that, because hopefully, you will instead find yourself four years down the line writing the words: 'In conclusion, it has been a pleasure to work with Miss Dove and although I shall be sad to lose her, she is ready for this exciting next move in her career...'

Chapter 8

Induction and training issues for new teachers

Edward Elliott

Teachers are a school's greatest resource, and most Heads will tell you that recruiting and retaining the best of them is one of the most important – if not *the* most important – aspects of their job. Any good school owes a duty to its staff, and its pupils, to ensure that new teachers are properly inducted and supported so that they can become effective from day one.

In the stress league, new jobs are right up there with getting married or moving home. Even experienced teachers who have become well established in their current schools can find themselves facing professional difficulties when they move to a new school where their lack of reputation can mean they are subject to unexpected classroom challenge. Your street-cred does not always follow you from a place where, over the years, you have become totally established, to one where you have to earn your spurs all over again.

Difficult pupils aside, all new teachers – whether experienced or not – will need to master the detail of their new schools, whether it be two-week timetables, variable lesson lengths, or the vagaries of school nomenclature, with dining halls becoming refectories and Year 11 rebranded as the upper fifth. On top of this, there is the need to learn (and remember) hundreds of pupil and adult names, and the requirement not to get lost between morning break in the staff room and period four in a room mysteriously known as SC1.

Given all these challenges, the need for proper induction programmes for all new staff is clear. What is remarkable is that for years many schools didn't have such programmes and new staff were largely left to sink or swim. Such a baptism of fire may have had its evolutionary uses in weeding out weaker teachers, but many now successful colleagues (myself included) only just survived their 'probationary' year.

I vividly remember my first term in teaching. One Friday I was helping to design bank notes for my previous employer: the next I was struggling with a Year 11 class, described with characteristic under-statement as 'a bit lively' by my then head of department. It was indeed quite a handful, and lacking a PGCE, I had to learn quickly and steeply on the job.

Only when the class found out about my prior life in the security print business, and mid-lesson breaks could revolve around how to spot counterfeit bank notes, did things improve. I have also heard of one new teacher who, in similar circumstances, told his class in desperation that he was a karate expert: fortunately for him, they never called his bluff!

Other new entrants were not so lucky, and although we all survived our first year, two left teaching shortly afterwards. In both cases their professional confidence had never taken root, and the prospect of continuing to teach children whom they had found difficult in year one pushed them out of the profession. Therein lies an important message: there are downstream consequences of a difficult first year, as staff doubt their own competencies and vocation, and pupil (and sometimes parent) gossip brands such colleagues as 'poor teachers' for years to come.

Things have moved on since the early 1990s. The arrival of the Training and Development Agency for Schools (TDA), the requirements of qualified teacher status (QTS), and the work of ISCtip have revolutionised new teacher induction. There is now a clearly-laid pathway for all post-initial teacher training (ITT) newly qualified teachers (NQTs) to follow in their first year, which includes a 10% timetable reduction; regular meetings with key staff involved in the induction process; an individualised and structured plan of support; clear schemes of learning to follow; and the opportunity to observe experienced colleagues at work.

While no such statutory requirements exist in the independent sector for those entering the profession without an ITT qualification, common sense dictates they should benefit from at least this level of support and monitoring, and in many cases they need more. The 33 Q standards set up by the TDA for the award of QTS and the 41 Core standards to be met by the end of induction certainly represent excellent benchmarks for all new teachers to attain.

Any chronology of new teacher induction needs to begin in the term *prior* to the start of employment. In the best scouting tradition, teachers need to be prepared – and for new entrants to the profession, this usually means being two weeks ahead of themselves with lesson planning and resource creation. Thus, when the inevitable flu bug strikes in November, the NQT can rest and recuperate without worrying too much about keeping ahead of his/her pupils.

However, to keep two weeks in front of classes means using some of the summer holiday to prepare materials. This in turn requires HoDs to be well organised and to spend time with NQTs going through schemes of learning and departmental resources in the summer term prior to a September start. In schools where teaching resources are now stored on an intranet, the new teacher will need access (preferably remote) to the school network before they start their contract. (Incidentally, this is a good reason why teachers' contracts should run from 1st August to 31st July.)

Summer term planning should also focus on the new teacher's timetable. Timetable in haste and repent at leisure, and great care needs to be taken to ensure new teachers are shielded from difficult classes (especially for late afternoon lessons), and that for paired teaching in the sixth form, sets are shared with an experienced colleague who will be a good source of advice and encouragement.

The summer term should also see the production of a new teachers' survival guide which includes all the essential bits from the much larger staff handbook with some top tips for making a success of the first fortnight. Any survival guide needs to be concise, or its impact will be lost. It does, however, need to include a copy of any staff code of conduct so that new colleagues are aware from day one of their professional duties and responsibilities.

It should never be forgotten that young new staff are often closer to sixth form students in age and outlook than they are to their teaching colleagues, and while this can be a strength, it also brings with it professional dangers. NQTs must be aware of the legal boundaries within which they operate (such as the Sexual Offences Act 2003), and from whom they should seek advice and assistance if they find themselves subject to the likes of a teenage crush.

There is a particular reminder implicit here to schools which like to chance their arm and to pick young and outgoing new teachers straight out of university without a teaching qualification. Never under-estimate how much guidance even the most brilliant of them *may* need in their first year, both in technical teaching terms and in other ways.

Plenty of potential grief can be saved by the right person gently pointing out that it is unwise to adopt the easy-going older brother or sister figure too much with the Year 10 class, and cautioning against clothes which are obviously more suited to recreational time than the professional world. A quiet but firm word from a different person at an early stage to the class concerned can be useful, too.

Careful thought needs to be given to which staff are involved in the new teacher induction process. A mix of skills and roles are required, and whilst the HoD will be central to the process as both the line manager and the subject specialist best able to measure progress against Core standards, others should be involved too.

In some cases this will be to bring specific expertise to the induction process (*eg* in child protection), but it should also be for supportive reasons, as many new teachers will prefer to discuss concerns first with another young teacher (perhaps in their second or third year) rather than going straight to their HoD. Such peer group mentoring can work very well, as it protects the HoD from dealing with every trivial worry, allows the NQT to be open and honest, and gives the young teacher mentor some early management experience. However the young teacher providing peer support needs to be trained, and must realise when s/he needs to involve the HoD.

The other benefit of having a range of staff involved in the induction process is that it exposes the new teacher to a wide variety of teaching ideas, approaches and styles. Occasionally, one reads of schools where there is an approved lesson format – a recipe that all colleagues are supposed to follow. While this might guarantee a minimum classroom standard, it comes at a high price. Pupils benefit from, and enjoy, a variety of teaching styles and they would lose out if all eight lessons in the school day were taught to some homogenised format.

Once a new teacher is *in situ*, induction can begin in earnest. Most schools will have some form of INSET before pupils return, and this time can be used in part to ensure that new teachers have a clear understanding of school and departmental procedures (vital where there are specific health and safety requirements to address: make sure, for example, that new staff teaching occasional games lessons are fully aware of what to do in the event of sports injury). It is also a good time to provide training in the school's ICT system and key software packages.

It can be tempting for new staff to go to ground at the beginning of term and burrow away in departmental offices, preparing lessons and resources. While this is commendable in many respects, it is also important for new teachers to spend time socialising with their colleagues and getting to know the rest of the common room. Little tips like sitting with different colleagues at lunch each day can aid the integration process.

Once term is under way, the induction process can proceed – both on a formal and informal basis. The formal process should run in accordance with published ISCtip guidelines and should include regular meetings with both the HoD (or subject tutor) and a senior member of staff (probably the induction tutor). These meetings need to be given quality, undisturbed time and should be regarded as sacrosanct.

Remember again that teachers are a school's greatest resource and time needs to be invested accordingly in their development. An individual programme for monitoring and support needs to be agreed with the new teacher, with clear targets and advice on how to reach them. This advice is likely to include the use of lesson observations (to examine best practice elsewhere in the school); attendance on specific training courses such as those organised by ISCtip and IPD; reading and reflection; trying new approaches to assessment; classroom management and teaching. There are lots of good, accessible books on teaching methods – one of my favourites is Sue Cowley's *Getting the Buggers to Behave* (Continuum, 2004).

Because of the centrality of the HoD in the induction process, new teacher induction can become very subject-orientated. Do not forget that some of the Core standards deal with issues which lie beyond the department, so whole-school training will be needed, most notably in pastoral matters, and heads of section should be fully involved in the induction process.

While the formal process lies in the obvious, documented part of induction, the informal process is equally valuable. By informal induction I mean all the casual observations, words of encouragement in passing, acts of kindness, and quiet words of advice that do not form part of any formal observations but which serve to motivate, encourage and shepherd new teachers in the right direction. Such acts help to cement departmental teams, build friendships, and breathe humanity into the NQT induction process.

New teachers need to be well prepared for major events in the school year such as parents' evenings, report writing, and public exams. Time spent preparing for them invariably saves time which may otherwise be spent in mopping up problems afterwards. Simple advice on parents' evening etiquette, including asking parents and pupils to declare their hands first ("How is little Jonny finding peri-glaciation?"), and postponing any difficult discussions to a subsequent meeting by which time emotions will have calmed, is invaluable.

In the same way, spending time analysing examples of good and bad reports and advising on any 'house style' is important. A poor parents' evening, or a batch of reports returned by the deputy head, can undermine any new teacher's professional confidence and can exacerbate stress levels at busy times.

Public exams are again something about which new teachers need to be fully briefed. They must be aware of the requirements of exam specifications, and in particular the dangers and temptations that surround coursework. Inexperienced teachers eager to please and do well for their pupils and school can easily find themselves over-stepping the exam board mark and offering too much help with coursework.

Other new teachers may not fully appreciate the need to both drill pupils in examination technique (*ie* in those specific catch phrases required to reach attainment level four in each subject), and to teach in a way that stimulates a real interest in the subject and a genuine love of learning. Many are understandably very cautious and play safe, focusing on examination technique, whilst just occasionally others will go in to

Dead Poets Society mode, ignoring the requirements of the exam board in order to satisfy the greater needs of the subject.

Any good induction programme should spot these problems at an early stage, and of course that is what induction is all about: identifying concerns before they become problems and helping new teachers address them.

In many ways the diagnostic part of induction is the straightforward one. Observations of lessons and pupil work provide evidence of problems, and if a constructive relationship of trust is established, many new teachers will discuss such problems openly with HoDs. What can sometimes be more challenging is getting new teachers to respond to problems in a productive fashion. Some will over-react to a problem such that the noisy lesson now becomes one of absolute silence.

The trickiest cases of all are 'new teacher perfectionists' and the 'deaf ears'. The 'new teacher perfectionists' will work 36 hours in a day to perfect resources and mark assessments with painstaking accuracy – but they generally drive themselves into the ground unless they can be convinced that corners have to be cut in order to survive and thrive in teaching. The 'deaf ears' teacher acknowledges problems, recognises solutions, but then doesn't seem to do anything about them. As a result the same problems and the same recommendations feature time and again in their written reviews.

Certain times of the year are particularly difficult for new teachers, and the induction process needs to be sensitive to these trouble spots. Generally, the first month in a new job goes well, and in this honeymoon period pupils are restrained in their classroom behaviour as they either settle into a new school themselves or take time to get the measure of their new teachers. Difficulties normally arise from week four onwards as pupils begin to test boundaries and teachers start to tire.

This is a critical time and the way in which such early difficulties are addressed often determines the success or otherwise of the induction year. As ever, HoDs should not be afraid to step in to nip problems in the bud, by using a sliding scale of intervention beginning with quiet words of advice to the new teacher, and ending with full scale lesson observation, where the HoD's presence can ensure pupil co-operation whilst making sure the new teacher has acted on those initial quiet words of advice.

Other times to watch out for include the end of term, when a combination of teacher fatigue and pupil excitement can lead to a premature loss of academic momentum and over-reliance on 'video lessons'. Never forget just how hard the first year or two of teaching can be, especially for the 22- or 23-year-old who is often having to adjust simultaneously to the dispersal of friends after graduation, the loss of the feeding, accommodation and laundry facilities of most universities and maybe life in a new relationship.

All this comes without the bank of files of teaching notes which those of us well-established in the profession have accumulated over many years. Try to ensure too that such teachers do not volunteer for *too* much during that first, crucial October half-term or Christmas holidays: they will be unusual if they do not need that time to catch up on sleep, and to re-charge batteries for the next set of challenges.

The improvements in new teacher induction have been substantial in recent years, and we have come a long way from the 'sink or survive'/'don't smile before Christmas' mentality of old. Such improvements are welcome and reflect a growing recognition that, since teachers are a school's greatest resource (and cost), they need to be developed through proper investment, training and support.

A school is only as good as its weakest teachers, though, and a proper induction process can do much to raise the standard of the lowest common denominator. The next challenge is to ensure that excellent first year induction schemes continue in subsequent years as part of a wider professional development programme.

Chapter 9

The learning styles phenomenon: reality or hoax?

Frances Green

According to the Dunn and Dunn learning-style model (1992/3/9), Learning Style is the way in which each learner begins to concentrate on, process, absorb and retain new and difficult information. How often have you watched in amazement as a colleague or friend has set about a task in a completely different way to you? If only they did it this way, (*ie* your way), you think, they would be so much more successful.

Teachers are particularly given to this way of thinking. Over the years they have developed expertise in certain areas, set particular tasks and found appropriate ways to complete them successfully. However, sitting in class will be many pupils with different approaches, and although their technique may not be the same, as long as the end result is successful, does it matter? Learning styles pay homage to these different approaches and a Learning to Learn Programme is a feature of many schools – particularly in the state sector.

The learning styles approach developed in the United States in the 1970s, when research on brain development was utilised by people such as Kolb who identified four main learning style types: the diverger, converger, accommodator and assimilator. When neurologist Roger Sperry won a Nobel Prize for demonstrating that the right and left hemispheres play distinct but complementary roles in adult brains, he triggered a plethora of self-help books, encouraging us to identify whether we had a left or right brain approach to life.

With the increased use of MRI scans scientists now know that there isn't a 'split' between the left and right brains. For example, it was generally considered that use of language was a purely left brain activity – but now it can be seen that language is, in simplistic terms, governed by both sides of the brain. However, as research continued apace in the medical world, educators embraced the concept too, and before long a whole range of brain-based learning techniques had evolved.

'If they can't learn the way we teach, then we must teach the way they learn.' So writes Gillian Wheeler in *Boys' Learning in MFL* (Specialist Schools and Academies Trust, 2007). Accelerated learning, the Accelerated Learning in primary schools (ALPS) approach, multiple intelligences and many more permutations of the new knowledge were to find their way into study skills courses. Teachers were made aware that their pupils had very different needs in class, and not all were comfortable with the concept.

Multiple Intelligences was one of the theories which probably impacted most on the curriculum. When Dr Howard Gardner suggested that there was more than one way to be intelligent, he threw a lifeline to many a struggling learner. The suggestion that we should celebrate the many talents or intelligences that a pupil might have was definitely appealing to many educators and parents.

Howard Gardner proposed that children had a range of intelligences: linguistic, logical/mathematical, musical, spatial, bodily/kinaesthetic, interpersonal, intrapersonal and naturalistic. Traditionally the linguistic and logical/mathematical intelligences were those most valued in schools and a student with strengths in these areas could be expected to do well.

Skills such as interpersonal and bodily/kinaesthetic, however, had hitherto not been so highly regarded. As with any 'new' theory, it was not without its critics and the most common criticism levelled is that it labels pupils – in this case with what might be a spurious intelligence. At least it is positive labelling, and surely it is better for pupils to celebrate (for instance) a bodily/kinaesthetic intelligence than to consider themselves hopeless?

On introducing the multiple intelligences quiz to a Year 9 class, Bethan and Hannah looked glum. "What's the point?" they said. "We're not intelligent". Having been coaxed into filling out the questionnaire, they both scored highly on interpersonal and bodily/kinaesthetic skills. Both pupils were in the netball team, part of the dance group and were reliable, hard-working girls in the house sports teams.

Yet in an education system that mainly celebrates logical and linguistic skills, they felt inadequate. In the world of business their keen interpersonal and organisational skills would be valued and, if it does nothing else, a multiple intelligences approach at least encourages pupils and staff to see that everyone has different, but equally valuable, skills.

So, one has to ask, is there any benefit in analysing a pupil's learning style? Only at the most simplistic level would you identify a pupil's learning preference as visual, auditory or kinaesthetic (VAK) as there is much more to a learning style than these three components. Many questionnaires, for example in accelerated learning course materials or questionnaires on the internet, do only assess VAK.

In fact, however, each 'style' can be subdivided into sub-categories. For example: is this a visual learner who learns best by reading, or one who responds better to information in diagrammatic form or on screen, or maybe a child who learns best by using internal visual skills, such as imagination or daydreaming? There is no doubt that there are many shades of learner and that each one will be unique.

For the HoD (and, indeed, each department member) the problem is how can (s)he possibly cater for so many different kinds of learning approach? Wouldn't it be better to stick to tried and tested methods? A frequent argument is: 'we didn't have learning styles when I was at school, we just got on with it and I've done OK'. It would be an exceptional person who went through their schooldays liking each teacher equally and getting the same amount of enjoyment from every lesson. We all have our preferences and this is what makes us individuals.

One also has to remember that teachers are in the category of 'super learners', in that they have turned learning into a full time occupation and are hopefully passing on their skills. Yet it is of particular benefit for teachers to identify both their own learning and teaching styles if they are to be even more effective in the classroom. While the majority of pupils will adapt well to a variety of classroom practices, some will find it difficult and using a learning styles assessment can form a useful basis for dialogue between teacher and pupil.

Finding a learning style inventory that works with pupils and provides all teachers, parents and pupils with useful information is slightly more difficult, not least because research into the brain continues apace and causes shifts in opinion. The Dunn and Prashnig system of learning-style analysis is one such example – completed online and providing a wealth of information.

Do using learning style assessments have any practical use in the classroom? In my own school, over 700 assessments have been completed during the period of use and it has proved informative on a number of levels. For example in Year 12 we had two biology groups which appeared to have completely different approaches to learning and whose teachers were finding the situation very perplexing. A group analysis revealed that the pupils did indeed appear to have very different styles.

Perhaps the most telling statistic was that group one comprised 25% who were strongly non-conformist and none who were strongly conformist while, in group two, 45% pupils were strongly conformist and none were non-conformist. Group one had a large proportion of holistic learners but in group two the majority had a more analytical approach. Even their preferred working environments were different, as 73% of group two wanted to work in silence while the majority of group one preferred to have sound while they worked. There were many more differences and the biology department then restructured its approach, with markedly successful results.

So what difference does it make whether a pupil has a sequential or holistic approach to learning? Take the example of the flat pack furniture: the logical learner will carefully enumerate all the parts and read the instructions, while the holistic processor will look at the picture on the outside of the box, shake all the bits onto the floor and hope to get to the finished product by one method or another. The logical learners on the whole prefer the no-nonsense, step-by-step approach, concentrating on the assignment: they do not like any divergence from the task. The holistic processor prefers a light humorous approach, being given the big picture first and won't mind if the teacher digresses and adds comments to illustrate the topic.

It came as a surprise to a member of the home economics department to learn that some pupils might just prefer to read through a recipe and follow the written instructions to work independently, rather than watching a demonstration. Explaining that some would prefer this approach, while some would like to listen to an explanation, and others would prefer to watch a demonstration, was perplexing. However, in one of the lessons the next day, the teacher gamely tried all these methods, and was surprised to find which pupils preferred which.

Reporting that the finished product was not so consistent, the teacher did admit that the girls had enjoyed the lesson and appreciated being allowed the freedom to experiment. Obviously it is not always practical to use this approach in class, but teachers would do well to remember that if they have a strong preference for delivering a lesson in a certain way, a single-method approach is not necessarily going to reach every pupil. Some pupils have poor listening skills, so a lesson that is all talk is going to pass many a pupil by. Similarly not all will have well-developed reading skills, and so a lesson that is about reading from a text book and then making notes is not going to be effective for all, either.

Uptake of information is not the only criterion: there are other factors of equal importance. For example, the best way to teach kinaesthetic learners is often debated: most pupils will have a preference for whether they sit still or move around while learning. Of equal importance is the need for snacks and drinks. Some children really do need to chew to concentrate, and a quick check around any classroom may reveal shredded cuffs, chewed pencils, nibbled nails *etc.*

For others the harsh light of a fluorescent tube (or indeed any bright light) is distracting. Watch whether your own children or pupils turn on every light as they enter a room, needing bright light to work, or conversely turn lights off and draw the curtains because they prefer a more subdued light. Temperature is also important, and for every child who needs a warm room, another will prefer cooler climes.

Perhaps one of the most important parts of a learning styles inventory is the section on attitudes and motivation. With course work playing such an important part at all levels, knowing whether your pupils are likely to finish on time or not is very useful. The Dunn and Prashnig Inventory indicates whether pupils are self-motivated and have good persistence in finishing work. Those with low levels of persistence can be encouraged toward their goals if the teacher knows from the outset that there might be a problem. Conformity and responsibility are also scored in the inventory and again these are useful facts to know.

However, the learning styles approach has not been without its critics. A popular misconception of the term 'learning style' is that it is an arbitrary label attached to a child in an effort to help him or her learn and, furthermore, it seems that many critics wilfully misrepresent what the phrase means. No less a commentator than Baroness Greenfield is reported to have said that the method of classifying pupils on the basis of learning styles is a waste of valuable time and resources. The debate goes on, but with growing concerns about boys' perceived underachievement, learning styles have recently come under closer national scrutiny.

Working in a girls' school, one is under no illusions about the need that girls have to talk. As they reach adolescence the desire to make connections with others is strong, and this will be particularly witnessed in Year 9. Girls need their 'best friend' to confide in, and often need to belong to a particular social group. This is when problems can arise for the pastoral team, as the girls jostle for position to align themselves with particular social groupings and can pick on those who do not conform.

Meanwhile, as boys hit adolescence and their testosterone levels rise, they appear to take the opposite route and become monosyllabic and anti-social. They may socialise with their friends but are equally likely to retire to their rooms to play computer games, listen to music or other such solitary occupations. Communication with family is often at an all time low.

Girls have a head start in the linguistic stakes from infancy when they will, on average, have two to three times more words in their vocabulary than boys. As Nicola Morgan observes in *Blame my Brain* (Walker Books, 2005), 'they are driven by a desire for connection with other girls – and with boys'. Perhaps one of the biggest differences between boys and girls is that girls strive to please the teacher, whereas boys do not find this so necessary. Girls also get more stressed in their desire to turn in the perfect piece of work, whereas a boy will often do what is necessary to get by. In class, girls will enjoy a good discussion and in mixed classes girls can dominate because of their superior verbal skills.

There will be other broad differences in approaches to learning, with boys perhaps displaying a particular liking for a logical slant to lessons, wanting a no-nonsense approach and paying attention to details, particularly if the topic is something technical. It has been suggested that details and lists are what lead boys, rather than girls, to become train and plane spotters.

Females, on the other hand, are supposedly multi-taskers, and indeed some girls do show strong multi-tasking traits. These are often the pupils who find it difficult to concentrate for long in class, because they have so many things going on inside their heads. This type of learner needs a fast-paced environment and shorter, engaging tasks. Conversely, males are supposedly renowned for their ability to only tackle one thing at a time – and in an educational environment this can be an advantage.

One of the most often-cited arguments by supporters of single sex education is the fact that girls mature earlier than boys and respond to different approaches in teaching. The debate will no doubt continue to rage as to whether single sex or mixed schools are best but some girls and some boys will undoubtedly perform better in a single sex environment.

Research from the University of London (*Single sex schooling*, Professor Diana Leonard, Sage, 2006) suggested that girls who attended single sex schools performed better not just at school but in the world of employment. The research did not suggest that single sex schools achieved higher academic results, but did find that they were more likely to suggest that pupils followed a course of study based on their specific talents rather than a choice based on gender stereotypes.

For the HoD the learning style assessments can be a useful tool, either as a group profile or the individual profiles of pupils. Such assessments can be used when monitoring progress, setting targets or monitoring grades. As another generalisation, pupils gain a stronger visual preference as they progress through the school, but this tends to be the seeing and watching preference rather than the reading preference.

Girls are also very strong in the kinaesthetic/emotion field; they need to feel good not only about themselves, but also about the subject and the teacher, to be successful and well motivated. Again in very general terms, boys do not seem to be so much influenced by the emotional side of education.

Individual assessments are useful as a basis for problem solving in the classroom (or, for that matter, outside it). With constant assessment in the curriculum, revision looms large in the academic life of the teenager. The phrase 'must revise more thoroughly' can strike terror into the hapless student's heart. What if you have revised as best you can, but to no avail? Time spent with the individual learning style analysis can give positive direction to revision: the appropriate senses to use for each subject (and they will differ from subject to subject); the best time of day; the environment; how long to work and who to work with.

Subject choice, particularly at sixth form level, is an especially difficult area. Weaker students (in the traditional areas of reading and writing) often want to try something different, maybe taking an 'ology' they haven't met before! However, learning-styles analysis can be a useful tool for both middle managers and class teachers in showing where the particular strengths of the student lie.

Linguists, for instance, will need good listening skills and the ability to talk and discuss as well as visual skills. Scientists will benefit from a sequential approach with good visual skills for symbols and diagrams and often will show a preference for hands-on learning. If a pupil starts to struggle with subject choices early in Year 12, checking the learning-styles analysis can be very beneficial. Moreover, this sort of assessment should not be overlooked when deciding on university and career choices and, when used in conjunction with, for instance, the Morrisby Test, can be a useful tool in refining choices.

For the hard-pressed subject teacher constraints of time and curriculum structure can pose limitations on trying anything new in class. A cross-curricular activity with lower school pupils can strongly favour audio/kinaesthetic styles of learning. For the pupils it can be a week in which they explore a single topic with lots of hands-on activities. For the teachers it is an opportunity to teach something which is not on the curriculum but which will extend the able pupil and boost the self esteem of those who may not be top of the class.

In addition it allows staff to 'try something different' without fear of failure. It is a learning curve for all and this, after all, is why we are all in school. Bertrand Russell suggested that no man can be a good teacher unless he has feelings of warm affection toward his pupils and a genuine desire to impart to them what he himself believes to be of value. Although some teachers may struggle to appreciate the usefulness of knowing a pupil's learning style, there is no doubt that the recognition that each child processes material in a different way, and may therefore approach learning tasks in a variety of styles, is a valuable lesson for all concerned.

Chapter 10

Heads of science

Nick Fisher

Running a science faculty can be one of the most rewarding times of your teaching career, though it is also time-consuming and exhausting. You are still at the sharp end of teaching, but your wider job has wonderful variety. It is my contention that heads of science have important responsibilities which extend far beyond merely running their department well, and providing exciting and effective teaching for the pupils who choose to study within it. There are exciting opportunities, too, to make the wider school community aware of scientific issues, and latest developments within the subject.

Why should the role involve explaining the importance of science within your school community? Questioning why a science education is important will also help us to develop our teaching strategies. So this is where I begin. In the early stages of 19th century public school education, science was considered to be a specialist extra on the curriculum and not an essential part of a pupil's classical education. Rugby was the first school in the country to introduce a compulsory science curriculum (1851), and Eton and Harrow followed soon after.

Since then the independent sector has often been involved in science curriculum developments which have had impact on the teaching of science in *all* schools. One only has to look at the Nuffield work in the '60s and '70s to see how significant that has been. Since then, science teaching in our schools has continued to be innovative, in the design of buildings, laboratories and specialist teaching classrooms, in equipment innovations and in curriculum developments and teaching methods.

Some pupils and parents believe that you study science only to become a scientist. But does everyone studying English or history become a professional writer or historian? No: one of the biggest employers of graduate and PhD scientists is the City, thanks to a scientist's transferable skills of analysis, team-working, computer literacy and problem-solving capabilities. To justify the place of science in the 21st century national curriculum you can also point to the obvious technological needs of our country and, indeed, the entire world – and the need to maintain and develop these further.

Science claims its place in the education of every pupil because of its immense cultural significance: it has transformed the world; shaped the course of history; radically altered religious belief; and profoundly influenced literature. It is integral to our cultural heritage and this should be celebrated. At the turn of the 20th century in France there was some anti-science propaganda linked to the military use of technology which had tarnished the reputation of science. Henri Poincare's response was succinct: 'It is only through science and art that civilisation is of value'.

Through studying science we transform our views of the universe, deepen our interpretations, change and gain new perspectives. Edgar Mitchell, who flew the Apollo 14 spacecraft to the moon, describes an epiphany he had on the way back to Earth:

> 'The biggest joy was on the way home. In my cockpit window every two minutes I would see the earth, the moon and the sun and the whole 360° degree panorama of the heavens. It was a powerful and overwhelming experience.
>
> 'And suddenly I realised that the molecules of my body, the molecules of the spacecraft, the molecules in the bodies of my partners, were prototyped and manufactured in some ancient generation of star. And there was an overwhelming sense of oneness, of connectedness. It wasn't them and us. It was me – that was all of it – it's all one thing. And it was accompanied by an ecstasy or a sense of "Oh my God, wow, yes!" – an insight, an epiphany.'

A poet would say we are made of stardust: a cynic would say we are nuclear waste. The Apollo astronauts were amongst the most highly trained scientists and pilots. It is not the man-made technology that got the men to the moon that was exciting, but the emotional (almost spiritual) realisation of how connected we are to the natural universe. In an age when emotional intelligence in teaching has become a high priority, we know that if pupils feel excited by science emotionally, they can engage their intellect. Sometimes the two play off each other.

Science can also touch emotions through its artistic dimension. The abstract developments in science during the late 19th and early 20th centuries with the birth of quantum mechanics and relativity coincided with the growth of the abstract art movements lead by Braque and Picasso. Jacob Bronowski described the situation well: "When it comes to atoms, language can be used only as in poetry. The poet too, is not nearly so concerned with describing facts as with creating images."

Artists too have taken an interest in and been spiritually moved by developments in science. Salvador Dali once declared: "And now the announcement of Watson and Crick about DNA. This is for me the real proof of the existence of God."

Science and the arts have many common themes. They include beauty, harmony and symmetry; experimentation with light and colour; use of imagery (poetry, models, ambiguity and duality); and revolutions and change, with the move towards greater abstraction in the last 100 years. But how often are these common themes highlighted in our teaching?

As both a literary man and a scientist, C P Snow was well equipped to write a book about science and the arts in the middle of the last century. In his 1959 book (and Rede lecture), *The Two Cultures and the Scientific Revolution*, he argues that practitioners of either science or the literary arts know little, if anything, about the other. He asserts that this is damaging for society. People have argued that his premise was wrong and that he, like others, did indeed find it possible to live in both the literary and scientific camps.

My experience of teaching students even today is that they still believe they have either an artistic or scientific leaning. This polarisation may well be intellectually damaging and limiting for our very brightest and most creative thinkers. Creativity in science is necessary if we are to have Galileos, Daltons, Darwins, Curies, Einsteins, Cricks and Watsons of the future.

The school curriculum can often compartmentalise knowledge. The differences between disciplines may be exaggerated and their similarities ignored. Appreciating the considerable similarities between art and science (and indeed the sciences) unlocks the potential for collaboration between teachers of both subjects, as well as enhancing pupils' education. Natalie Angier's book *The Canon: The Beautiful Basics of Science* illuminates how biology, chemistry and physics have transformed our view of the universe and ourselves.

So how should we teach science? To present it merely as facts to be learned is to do both it, and our pupils, a great disservice. Pupils come into lessons with many ideas about the natural world – some of them intuitive, some learnt and many that do not fit with accepted scientific knowledge. Much of this knowledge has taken centuries to develop, so it is important that we do not stifle confidence simply by telling pupils they have misconceptions and that they have got the wrong end of the stick.

Some of the best scientists experienced similar difficulties. We must accept there are alternative viewpoints that pupils have that could be valid. We need to get pupils to think about a phenomenon in a different way to transform their interpretations – and this demands more than didactic teaching: it requires discussion of the alternative viewpoints.

Practical experience is also essential: it can help challenge pupils' interpretations of the world and help guide them towards the accepted scientific view. But practical work in a school environment is only useful if pupils are engaged with it and are genuinely thinking. I sometimes question whether it is used simply to punctuate a lesson, to give the teacher a breather and the pupils a rest from listening to the teacher.

The hands-on approach is important, but it is also essential that pupils' minds are kept on the science: hence the need to motivate the thinking process before, during and after any practical work. If you examine the work of a professional scientist, what proportion of their time would be spent on practical work? There is far more time spent reading literature, planning an experiment with colleagues, presenting arguments to obtain funding, and analysing and evaluating the final project work.

Science progresses quite slowly, and even revolutions can be gradual and painstaking. Should we make science appear as exciting as it is, or *more* exciting? As a recruiting exercise, there has been a tendency to promote science through excitement. Some university departments and government-funded initiatives have tried to promote it through exciting lectures with dramatic demonstrations and audience participation. I have nothing against this and I use dramatic whizzes and bangs as much as possible. But if this is all there is, it can just turn the brightest students right off.

Science is a hard intellectual and cerebrally satisfying set of subjects. Countries need a core of outstanding scientists as well as the good ones, so we need to recruit the brightest to cope with the intellectual demands required in a modern technological and ethically challenging society. But science is competing with intellectually stretching subjects such as history.

You can write an excellent essay in history that really goes beyond the boundaries of an examination. Not so easy with science to write an original piece of work – unless you give pupils some opportunities to engage in ethical debates, and to explore unknown territory with genuine open-ended practical investigations. The recent Cambridge Pre-U curriculum development has addressed this issue by introducing personalised research into some of its syllabuses.

For some pupils, there is a great benefit in exploring the historical context of physical theories to open up debate and creative thinking about science. The Perspectives on Science course (developed since 2000) illustrates the human face of the subject through discussion and thinking critically, so important in the world of scientific research.

It equips students to analyse profound and exciting historical, philosophical and ethical questions, and it culminates in a 5000 word dissertation and *viva voce* exam which brings to the fore the important skills of literature search, cross-referencing, balanced argument and communication that all good scientists need. So, through science we can get pupils to learn new ways of thinking about the world. This can be as challenging and rewarding as analysing the subtleties of poetry in English lessons.

And management of a science faculty varies greatly from one school to another, even within the independent sector. In some schools, the role of the head of science may be simply that of an administrator, entering candidates for public exams; in others it will range much more widely.

Some schools may have separate biology, chemistry and physics buildings, making it difficult to co-ordinate formal collaboration and informal discussion; in others there is a shared building and the head of science runs all aspects, including timetabling, allocating specialist rooms and managing the whole budget.

In essence, however, the job has the same aims and makes the same demands in any school. These will include communication with the senior management and with parents; management of teaching staff; choosing an appropriate curriculum; teaching issues; pupil issues; links with the wider community; results and accountability. But it also involves extra responsibilities that do not come with running English, maths or history: management of a budget for both equipment and consumable items (chemicals, *etc.*); further dimensions in health and safety; co-ordination of at least three subjects (biology, chemistry, physics and possibly other subjects such as astronomy, geology, *etc*); communication with equipment manufacturers; management (and appraisal) of heads of subject and technical staff and the recruitment of the latter; and allocation of laboratory space.

It is vital that the Head is aware of the appropriate financial investment required for teaching science in your school. It is not just the laboratory space, capital equipment, and costs of chemicals and other consumables, but also training costs to stay on top of health and safety issues. Then there is the cost of technical support. Without this you can not maintain equipment and deliver a successful scientific experience with the right balance of stimulating practical and demonstration work.

In some schools there is a separate budget for each of biology, chemistry and physics. In others the science budget covers the whole faculty and the head of science allocates expenditure where it is needed. Requests for capital equipment come from the heads of department. An over-view is important; in many cases equipment can be shared between departments, with a cost saving for the school. An unpredicted and necessary over-spend in one department can also be offset by an under-spend in another. The latter is particularly useful as bursars are often reluctant to allow budget saving from one financial year to feed the payment for expensive equipment in the following year.

One of the major roles is communication with senior management, parents and governors about the curriculum and strategic vision for the faculty as a whole. Some of this can often be done through websites, but the personal touch is still of major importance. Representing the science faculty in events and presentations to parents at open days and parents' meetings is a public relations exercise that is important and may demand much of your time.

But the key role is that of managing your staff: everyone from your heads of biology, chemistry and physics and your teachers who may have other responsibilities in the wider school arena, to technicians, administrative staff, the cleaners and laboratory assistants. A shared vision has to be developed. Talents and enthusiasms have to be encouraged and nurtured through discussion. Be sensitive to the creative vision of others, while trying to spread good practice and maintaining some sense of consistency and impartiality. Encourage initiative.

The career development of teachers must be seen as a major part of your role as head of science. Although science teachers are precious personnel whom we usually want to hold on to, it is our duty as heads of science to support teachers in moving on to heads of department roles in other schools and technicians to move on into science teaching careers. If you are fortunate enough to be able to attract good replacements, you can keep your science faculty dynamic and alive with fresh ideas.

Collaboration can be enhanced in the design of the science area. If there is a single building you are very fortunate: if you can avoid teachers having their own dedicated laboratory, even better. Although there are advantages for individual teachers in having their own laboratories, this can lead to isolation and a lack of unity. Informal discussion and sharing of ideas happens naturally if teachers have to retreat to a shared administrative base between lessons.

For collaboration on a more formal footing, chairing weekly meetings with the three separate heads of individual sciences is a necessity. It can be more productive than trying to meet too frequently with the whole faculty (including technicians) and it helps to set agendas for big issues on which the whole faculty may need to be consulted. This two-tier approach to meetings, along with regular termly gatherings of all the science teachers and technicians, should promote an *esprit de corps* that can help generate creativity and a shared vision. It also enables you to monitor delegated tasks.

Staff will be enthusiastic about attending only if they feel they have some input and their voice will be heard (and responded to positively!). Often these meetings are not timetabled but occur out of normal school time. Keep them brief. Send out an agenda to staff in advance to give them an opportunity to think. If you have a large faculty, consider splitting it into groups with an appointed spokesperson (cross-curricular, with biologists, chemists and physicists sharing ideas together) followed by a plenary session. Any matters agreed and matters for action should be published in as concise a form as possible and distributed to all science staff, again including technicians. Important matters for action should always be sent to an appropriate member of the SMT for further discussion.

Mutual INSET within the science faculty can often provide far better value than an external training course. Cross-curricular INSET between science and maths and ICT departments is also very beneficial. Set aside time for teachers to teach each other. There are no travel costs and no time-wasting in travelling and the focus is usually more appropriate to what is needed. You can throw money at a science department buying new equipment, but if there is no time to practise using it, the dust will find a good home on which to settle.

You can further encourage the cross-fertilisation of ideas between science subjects through developing public understanding for science lectures and other special events in pairs; and curriculum development with examination boards and universities. It is also good for teachers teaching more than one science subject to help bring out cross-curricular links and to highlight differences and similarities between the subjects. However, we must still give teachers the opportunity to teach their specialist subject because it is only then that they can share their passion and enthusiasm effectively.

I have found that curriculum development is a very effective way of getting staff to collaborate and share ideas. It often involves technicians working closely with teachers and enhances team spirit. It helps teachers to maintain enthusiasm for their job, and it promotes the face of science positively to pupils. It helps to generate enthusiasm amongst teachers and technicians and to maintain lively debate and discussion. An infectious enthusiasm for science and for teaching will also help paper over any cracks!

Continuing professional development of staff is important in all departments. One of the biggest distinctions between science teaching and many other subjects is the demands of practical and demonstration work which present a whole host of extra issues to resolve. Good practical activities that stimulate students to think and demonstrations that help illuminate ideas require time to develop and to rehearse.

In some of the larger independent schools there is enormous pressure on staff to be out on the sports field and to contribute in other extra-curricular areas as well as pastorally. This all takes free time away from conscientious science teachers who want to improve their repertoire of practical and demonstration work. Ideally they should have at least a couple of lessons off each week to practise, although the budgets of many schools will not stretch to this. In addition, ideas and experiments sometimes need to be trialled in the holidays. Successful dynamic departments have teachers who devote time to developing new apparatus and trying out new ideas with existing kit.

It is important for a head of science to watch all the staff teach. It is also important for this to be reciprocated! Lesson observation in science should be seen as a way of sharing expertise and one of the most important aspects of continuing professional development. Encourage staff to observe a 'buddy teacher' teaching a challenging set, possibly a set that you share (if you have streaming in science); to observe a colleague using new software, equipment or a new teaching method, and to team teach a set, particularly when arranging a range of different activities for group work.

Some staff may be defensive at the prospect of this. The least threatening approach is to encourage staff to observe something positive in the lesson that they will take away and incorporate in their own teaching. Aim for at least a degree of informality: making notes and treating the exercise like a mini-inspection will reduce its effectiveness. However, it is sensible to agree in advance some desired outcomes and to ensure time is set aside afterwards to discuss things. The ensuing discussions from such positive and upbeat observations should form suitable dialogue to enhance the teaching of both teachers.

Most teachers are good performers and, when observed, they can ratchet up their stand-up routine to an impressive level. So, as an observer, I am always looking to see what the pupils are doing in class. There is nothing wrong with pupils being engaged by clear and enthusiastic delivery by a 'sage on the stage'. However it is worth asking to what extent the pupils are actively thinking?

Are there opportunities for them to discuss and explore ideas for themselves or are they being overly directed through question and answer sessions led by the teacher? Auditing a cross-section of lessons in one period can be a very efficient way of seeing whether there is a range of different activities being used in your department. Try to visit a class for just five minutes to observe what the pupils are engaged in before moving on to the next class.

Consider carefully who teaches your younger pupils. These will be the sixth formers in a few years time. Much research suggests that pupils start deciding whether they would like to go further with science when they are in Key Stage 3. The implication is that if we want to recruit we should be giving our most engaging and gifted teachers at least some lower school teaching.

All science teachers rely hugely on good technicians. This additional burden of cost in salary can be reduced if they can work in more than one discipline, but for a big faculty with a lot of practical work, a specialist dedicated to each subject area is a necessity. Their work can range from storage and deployment of equipment to repair work and development of new equipment. Independent schools have played a key role in developing apparatus over the past century. Nuffield science curriculum development in earlier decades involved the design and trialling of apparatus by teachers and technicians in close collaboration.

Technicians' views need to be sought regarding any changes to timetabling, allocation of laboratory space, budget for equipment and consumables and curriculum issues that may impact on the nature and extent of practical work. Include all your technicians in department meetings: you will also get a far better performance from them if they can be really involved in demonstrating and assisting with practical work in the classroom. You will also find that they will suggest improvements in your delivery that you will not have spotted!

Recruitment of technicians can be difficult and there needs to be a balance of maturity and experience with the young and trainable. The lack of apprenticeships in industry, redundancy and early retirement can all help in the recruitment of good quality technical staff. Thereafter they need to be nurtured and trained. In-house training requires time, and providing time in the week for this is a necessity. In schools where afternoons mean all pupils doing sport and the labs being empty there is a good opportunity for this.

However it only works well if suitable staff, such as the head of subject, can be involved. There tends to be a clash with the wider needs of the school demanding teachers to be on the touchline. Collaborating with local schools and organising informal INSET days for technicians during normal school time or during the early part of the school holidays can also be very profitable for boosting morale and raising standards in your technical team.

Then there is the problem of retaining good technical staff. This can only happen through a career structure of increased responsibilities – and with it a salary structure to reflect this. This involves performance management and the added workload to heads of faculty of appraisal. The hours of work in independent schools will often be very unsympathetic to the family life of a technician. In some of our schools there is a vast array of practical equipment, and much maintenance time is needed.

In such cases, it may be necessary to be flexible with working routines, for example by employing job-sharing schemes or time off *in lieu*. Here the bursar may need to be involved in maintaining some consistency in working conditions for all non-teaching staff. This may take a bit of negotiating! Be prepared for genuine puzzlement from new human resource teams who may not be familiar with the complexity of it all!

Pupils are, of course, the rationale for, and centre of, our work. Different subjects have varying conceptual problems and science subjects have many, some unique to science. Some students just will never reach the cognitive stage of development where ratio, direct proportion or rates of change have much meaning. Theoretical science which has limited concrete examples may prove a difficult area for many.

Wherever possible, the use of all senses – sight, touch, hearing, smell and taste – will help students to understand abstract concepts. The use of models and practical exercises will help reinforce these abstract ideas. Contextualising the science may also help to motivate pupils' learning and this is where the Salters' curriculum developments have been very successful.

Setting is highly desirable for teachers to help pitch their lessons at the right level of support and enrichment. Pupils develop at different rates and it is important to re-set each year to keep pace with this. But, rather than setting biology, chemistry and physics separately in Key Stage 3 and 4, consider streaming. This provides a huge benefit where the teachers of these three subjects share the same distribution of pupils. Discussions about teaching issues right across science disciplines will occur naturally and out of necessity. Issues of how to stretch the gifted, and how to support those who are struggling, can be aired and solutions shared.

Pupils who are very able or highly motivated need enhancements through open-ended tasks in lessons and preps and through extra-curricular enrichment. The extra-curricular work could include any or all of Olympiad exams; science discussion and debating societies; lecture societies where guests from universities and industry are invited to speak; seminars and workshop days; essay competitions; visits to universities; field trips; and even science-based plays. Michael Frayn's *Copenhagen* is a superb vehicle for showing how scientists often wrestle with political and emotional problems in their work. It shows that science is not isolated from personality.

Inviting good speakers from universities has become easier over the years as universities aim to promote themselves and their courses and provide outreach activities. However, lecturers are not always the best judges of what interests and motivates pupils; we are the experts in this field. Teachers putting together lectures on a range of cross-curricular and off-the-syllabus themes have helped to enhance our extra-curricular programme at Rugby and provide opportunities to collaborate with local schools.

Lecture titles have included Genetics and Free Will, Time Travel for Beginners, Surviving a Nuclear Attack, The Art of Science, Einstein's Nobel Prize, Biology of Love, The Sixth Sense, The Science of Superheroes, The Search for ET, Triangles in the Sky, and Chemical and Biological Warfare. Nothing but positive benefit has come from this hard work, and once developed, these lectures can be repeated annually. The material can be passed on to junior teachers for updating and to ensure that the good ideas are preserved for the future when staff move on to other schools.

Science field trips and expeditions have been increasingly squeezed out of the curriculum due to pressure from module exams. We need to fight quite hard to re-instate their importance, because there are obvious benefits to pupils when they can experience the connections between the theoretical parts of the curriculum and the real world. Furthermore, the need for observation in the field and relationships with the environment is a very important part of some aspects of science.

The modular examination system has forced many subjects to compartmentalise knowledge, whereas field studies require a more holistic connected approach. 'Joined-up' ideas and decisions made based on connections are essential not just to appreciate science itself but to enable pupils to have the experience of making decisions which require inputs from more than one source. Other spin-off benefits include team-building between pupils; improving student and teacher relationships; and pupils meeting professional scientists in the field – which in turn can help them to explore possible careers with the subject.

Links with the wider community and public benefit are issues for all independent schools these days, and heads of science might consider to what extent they can help in this. Sixth form pupils from our school have worked as mentors for gifted pupils at local state schools. Their mentoring involves them participating and assisting with teaching in support maths lessons, science laboratory classes and also in an after-school science homework club.

You could even consider peer mentoring within your own school of course! But one of the greatest benefits in partnerships with other schools is the opportunity for informal inspections and sharing best practice. It was partly by observing teachers in state schools using interactive whiteboards that I was convinced that we should introduce them in our own laboratories. Collaborations should never be considered patronising and my experience is that the benefits are always two-way.

Finally there are issues about measuring success, results and accountability. Monitoring the academic performance of all pupils is an important part of the job. This will include maintaining a database of all internal and public exam results and following up issues with tutors, parents and pupils. Are league tables credible these days with the confusions caused by module re-takes, and the differences in standard between different qualifications such as IB and other international examinations? We have all succumbed to the temptation to spin success with statistics.

Value added measurements will be important to your senior management team. Comparison of GCSE and A levels with Yellis and ALIS predictions can help you to demonstrate your success and provide academic targets. However there are less conventional ways in which we can judge the extent to which we are successful. Here are some questions to help you make a judgement about the success of your science faculty:

- How many pupils choose to study single science at GCSE (if offered as an option), science subjects in the sixth form, and science at university?
- How many pupils *voluntarily* attend extra-curricular events?
- Are your teachers and technicians happy?
- Are your teachers finding time to rehearse practical activities and demonstrations?
- Are teachers involved in any curriculum development – internally or nationally?
- Are any teachers involved in examination work?
- Are teachers and technicians sharing ideas within departments and between departments?
- How many teachers are willing to give up extra time for pupils outside class, whether for academic clinics or extra-curricular societies?

- How many teachers contribute to life outside the science faculty and to what extent?
- Is there any two-way collaboration with local schools (maintained, independent senior schools, or preparatory schools)?

These are not questions you would necessarily use to formally inspect departments, but the list may help you recognise whether there is anything really special happening in your science faculty. And to end where I began: being head of science is wonderfully varied work.

Chapter 11

ICT across the curriculum

Kathryn Macaulay

Enabling the delivery of ICT across the curriculum is not just about resourcing live lessons. Success in the implementation of a quality ICT curriculum delivery strategy is achieved when all the sectors within a school have continuing and full ownership of its development. High quality management of strategy underpinned by good short-term operational development planning enables the integrated provision of appropriate, successful curricular ICT use.

The past decade has seen extraordinary national development in ICT education. Government has committed copious investment to the thrust to realise e-confident, e-mature schools. In the funding debate ICT has been identified as being hugely important to the future of schools. Department for Children, Schools & Families (DCSF) research has shown that the use of ICT has a significant, motivational effect on pupils' learning and has an essential role to play in the provision of infrastructure and resources to support effective teaching and learning.

BECTA's report, *The Impact of ICT in Schools* (January 2007), is thorough in its description of the philosophy, accepted wisdom and outcomes of the years of investment and development. Tracking early use of ICT across the curriculum, it states that: 'Given the novelty value of computers in the '80s and early '90s, and limited access out of school, access to a computer was perceived as motivating in itself and used to promote pupil engagement in the learning process and ease classroom management in a relatively crude manner.

'By contrast, current use can be broadly described as characterised by collaborative, investigative and problem-solving activities designed to develop increasingly independent learners who are confident users of ICT, exploring and finding out for themselves, with greater peer interaction compared to non-ICT lessons.'

Successfully integrated, the use of this new and exciting tool has motivated pupils, increased the effectiveness of teaching and learning, enabled enjoyment, independence and collaboration, and provided opportunity for increased creativity and learning outcomes. With powerful strategies such as the £45bn Building Schools for the Future and Get a Next Generation Learning programmes, the government is unfailing in its commitment to funding ICT development. However *The Times* (15th April, 2008) reported that research from BECTA (the government's schools ICT advisory body), has acknowledged that although schools were spending £1bn on information technology each year, a staggering 80 per cent had not succeeded in making full use of it.

The individual, independent composition of schools is an enduring issue whenever national and local educational strategy is under review. This is most evident in the independent sector where schools have long needed to combine business strategy with the delivery of education and indeed the satisfaction of community. The assertion that there is no overall blueprint for a successful school is a matter for debate. What *is* clear, however, is that the unique and particular needs of pupils, staff and parents and the resources available in different schools ensure that a 'one size fits all' approach to ICT strategy is not possible to realise.

While independent schools may not have the very substantial ICT funding available to the maintained sector, it is important to remember that financial investment alone will not ensure excellent ICT provision. Independent schools are highly successful in their ability to choose their own strategy; they can rapidly respond to changing needs and are capable of providing an exceptionally flexible and targeted response to the needs of stakeholders and partners. These factors, matched with excellence in senior and middle management and a high level of investment in human and physical resources, can provide an outstanding infrastructure to channel ICT across the whole curriculum.

What facets of ICT need to be channelled? QCA schemes of work define ICT as the computing and communications facilities and features that variously support teaching, learning and a range of activities in education. The use of the word 'variously' in the QCA definition is a powerful one. It is very important to acknowledge the symbiotic relationship between the non-curricular, supportive, enabling ICT infrastructure provision and the ICT knowledge, skills and understanding delivery inherent in the process of teaching and learning. The two form the inter-dependent system of support and delivery of the many processes of the business of education.

Nicholas Carr, in his book *Does IT Matter?* (Harvard Business School Press, 2003), identifies IT as similar to 'older technologies' such as electric power in its maturing from innovative resource to standard infrastructure. There is much to be learnt from business and economic strategy in the management of commodities and resources in schools. However, education is not a true commercial business.

Although success is achieved with central focus on the ICT needs of the 'customers', our pupils – who represent the young people who will be the future – are not cloned or mass produced. A flexible and unique approach to the strategy of the business of education is needed, and this is one which independent schools can each successfully provide.

IT is the study or use of systems such as computers and telecommunications for storing, retrieving, and sending information. Business strategists would argue that there are two types of IT. One is the business of IT and the other is the IT of business. Defined in an educational context this would be described as comprising the ICT to enable teaching and learning and the teaching and learning of ICT.

Excellent infrastructure and reliable systems must assure heads of departments that the delivery of teaching and learning using ICT will be successfully supported in the real environment of the classroom. There is nothing more soul-destroying to enthusiastic able teams of staff than the failed implementation of well-planned schemes of work. Time is precious in a teaching scheme and cannot be wasted. Without secure ICT infrastructure provision and ongoing commitment to appropriate investment there can be little success. There is no quick win.

Successful ICT curricular delivery is a consequence of any senior management team's ownership of the whole school ICT strategic plan framework and development plan. The senior management team (SMT) should lead by example, and should be evident in their ability to practise what they preach. In the publication *ICT in primary and secondary schools: OFSTED's findings 2005/07* it is reported that 'The commitment from senior leadership teams is crucial. More commonly, there were shortcomings in the strategic leadership of ICT. This had a negative impact on all aspects of provision, including infrastructure, curriculum and, most importantly, achievement and standards'.

The constituent role of the technical manager of infrastructure provision, variously described as a manager of information services, technical services or network services, must be fully integrated into the strategic analysis, planning and development process. This person also has invaluable day-to-day knowledge of incident and problem management and is at the coal face of user interaction. Success is achieved when the school's management structure is flexible enough to enable contribution from, and ownership of, staff working at all levels in the organisation.

The style of middle and senior management structure within a school is a determining factor in the achievement of ICT strategic success. Yet in many ways it is the HoDs, working with all curricular and non-curricular staff teams, who are key ICT strategists and they in turn are the means by which the SMT develops a whole-school perspective. However, it is the HoDs who hold the immediate authority and accountability for the appropriate fulfilment of the pupils' (and the school's) ICT needs.

The staff development and training investment needed for successful organisations is very high, and the absence of sufficient provision of high quality ICT staff training in some independent schools has been highlighted by their inspection reports. Schemes of work and core ICT skills teaching have developed similarly in some, but not all, schools. Yet this is not just an independent school issue: ICT staff training in maintained schools has not always been well directed, either. Pockets of excellence are evident across both sectors, but they are not yet the norm.

Newly qualified teachers enter the profession these days with a range of basic ICT capabilities already acquired. Many schools have basic ICT training as part of new staff induction, and it is wise for standard expectations to be made clear both at interview and in staff handbooks. Acceptable use policies should be in place, and responsible email practice must be checked frequently. ICT resource should not be provided without appropriate evaluation of competence or appropriate training.

When new technology is a school-wide innovation, for example in the introduction of new reporting systems, all staff need to be included in compulsory INSET training. This applies to office and relevant support staff as well as teachers. Care must be taken in the planning and development of ICT staff training programmes to ensure quality in terms of content, delivery, allocation of sufficient time early in the day (the best time for skill acquisition), ongoing support provision and dovetailing with actual ICT resource provision.

With senior management commitment to investment in staff training and appropriate financial and time resourcing, it is possible to plan and deliver effective ICT staff training. There is no doubt though that a bold, creative and flexible approach is needed. It is not acceptable to merely 'tick the boxes' of training delivery. Long-term commitment to a well-supported, ongoing investment in an ICT staff development programme is necessary. Short sharp ICT training inputs benefit only a very small proportion of self-supporting members of staff. As Wendy Dubit of Vergant Media puts it: 'Teachers may be the most important workforce in the world, [but] our youth and our future are in their hands.' (www.vergant.com/speech.pdf)

After all, we must never forget that teaching and learning are the business of the school. Resourcing this core business is based upon satisfaction of need, and the staff must be able fully to own its development. The systems that are introduced should eventually enable as much departmental ownership of ICT as is possible. The power of ICT information, management and ownership must lie with the specialists – the HoDs – like other essential commodity resourcing, with appropriate infrastructure and senior management system management.

ICT investment is costly and must be ongoing for quality to be achieved. Funding issues can seem very demanding and new resources, when initiated, do not just have an initial one-off cost: there is also a replacement cost. A high quality, effective and well-managed three-year ICT strategy will have its own momentum and needs full commitment, resourcing and ownership at all levels of management in the school. Essential staff training should be symbiotic with ongoing ICT development and must be considered as part of the whole cost.

What ICT should we teach to our pupils, and how do we enable ICT teaching to flourish? What aspects of IT and ICT are central to the business of the school? How do these shape strategy and drive the need for development? The curriculum is not just the long list of timetabled and extra-curricular subjects studied by the pupil. It includes the 'hidden' knowledge, skills and understanding key to the creation of the 'whole' person. Central to the business of a school is the preparation of the young person for a future life. Prediction of future need fuels debate as to the correct 'positioning' of ICT in the rich experience we give our pupils.

Timetabled ICT lessons are essential to deliver core relevant skills, knowledge and understanding to pupils but we do not need to 'drill' pupils in the use of ICT. The comparison can be made with the development of numeracy and literacy skills, in both core and co-curricular context across the key stages. Skill acquisition in a co-curricular context is possible with effective timetable and cross-curricular co-ordination. Remember too that in recent years the global technology has advanced at an extraordinary pace, and for many (but not all) of our pupils, home provision of ICT is running at a high level.

Basic and intermediate Microsoft Office, email and internet skills were the essential capabilities of the early 1990s, but these are regarded now as a norm in the definition of basic, entry level ICT capability. It is widely acknowledged that all pupils should be offered the opportunity to develop basic, intermediate and advanced core ICT skills but the evidence of ICT core skills attainment at advanced level is less evident in many schools. Most pupils are capable of attaining these but the opportunity is not always there. Careful planning and integration can see these skills support the teaching and learning of so many subjects.

Following the years of huge investment in ICT in schools, OFSTED reported in 2007 that in secondary schools there was 'an overemphasis on developing students' communication and presentation skills. There were missed opportunities for students to understand and use the more complex features of standard software. Additionally, opportunities for students to acquire higher order ICT capability through their work in other subjects were too limited in many of the schools'.

At the time of writing (2008), national agencies (QCA, DCSF, BECTA) have been active in seizing opportunities offered by the rapid development of the emerging and converging global technologies to the great benefit of education in the UK. Less evident has been a review and enrichment of an aged and dry core ICT national curriculum and certification which gives employers and further education poor foundation for future needs. In fact 'the need to raise the debate about the repertoire of skills and approaches required by the education workforce in a modern education system' was highlighted by BECTA's *Harnessing Technology Review* in 2007.

Above all, there is a need (through QCA) to rethink our approach to what should constitute future ICT core skill development, and to create a situation which truly satisfies the present and future needs of pupils in all schools. The will to embrace review is evident, and change is needed to provide a challenging, high-level core skills programme of study fit for this future, very different from the one envisaged in the 1990s. There are some very good qualifications available, but few exist that reflect relevant future achievement at a really high level. Great possibilities lie ahead for the delivery of core ICT teaching skills and the acquisition of qualifications, if only we can get this issue right.

With the establishment of the first phase of the national roll-out of virtual learning environments, the continuing debate on the need for mobile learning devices and e-portfolios, we await the next big ICT 'idea' for the e-confident school. Meanwhile the ability to create communication documents will always be central to social and business communication locally, nationally and globally. With the emergence of 3D technologies and the use of virtual worlds, online learning will reinvent itself once again.

The use of virtual worlds such as Second Life as a learning experience is on the verge of mainstream appearance, with the UK taking a prominent role in the 'learning of how to learn' in a multi-user virtual environment (MUVE). Although it will be a while before such practice is the accepted norm in the UK and Europe, we must monitor MUVEs as the opportunities become viable realities.

The use of virtual learning space, such as that provided by Adobe Connect, has proved to be highly effective amongst staff, pupils and parents. The future will provide the ability to host secure personal spaces, where 3D interactive learning will provide exciting, flexible and creative environments in which to collaborate and mature. Pupils need to be able to produce high level communication media using advanced core ICT skills, as well as being well grounded in basic traditional document techniques.

Schools should closely follow materialising future technologies to create a proactive, appropriate management structure that allows change to be resourced at a speed effective for our pupils' needs. As new technologies emerge and converge, our strategies need to be creative and flexible, to allow for mobile device, email, web and other digital media to be used in presentation, communication and learning environments. In this way schools will integrate the ICT skills appropriate to the needs of subjects and deliver the higher level enriched core skills to empower their pupils for their future.

Although it sometimes seems that technology changes our lives and our society, the power of choice is still with us, and technology provides us with tools for the new work. The richness of our cultures, our visions and experiences, our knowledge and ability give us the foundation of the skills and wisdom we need to pass on. The focus should not be on the technology, but on the people using it. Good ICT provision is about their needs, their purpose and their ability to work together in community and partnership for the future.

Chapter 12

Meetings

Alice Phillips

You may be fortunate enough to inherit a department where all the members are fantastic practitioners; teaching inspirational lessons throughout every day; setting work and marking it within 24 hours of its being handed in; leading endless field trips or visits; generating huge numbers in your subject in the sixth form; communicating fully at all times with you and with each other; volunteering to do many extra hours assisting you with the administration of the department; endlessly supportive of each other; sharing all the resources they generate; never having *any* differences of opinion about school, departmental or even government educational policy. If you are, listen very carefully for the dull flapping noise of the pigs overhead.

It is far more likely that you are leading a team of dynamic and interesting individuals who all bring different strengths to your departmental table, but who also have different agendas, both for the subject, and in their own lives beyond their working day. In order to make the best of them and to create a cohesive and powerful departmental unit, you will have to hold regular meetings in order to build a strong team, whose members are aware of, and contribute to, the department's aims and objectives, and who work to support them.

It is a truth universally acknowledged that at the mere mention of the word *meeting*, most teachers go into, at best, a reluctant agreement that they are a necessary evil or, at worst, develop a hostile refusal to play ball at all. How often have we heard the muttering from the older members of the staff room: "I can't see the point in the whole staff discussing X", where X is possibly something as insignificant as the whole school development plan!

It is therefore wise to remember that the different generations of teacher in your department have grown up in a profession that has changed markedly from the hierarchical model of the dictator Head – whether benign or otherwise – into today's flatter, more inclusive and consultative approach, and all stations in between.

Your first job, therefore, is to decide what kind of meetings you will hold, and what atmosphere you will seek to create in them as head of the department. Will they merely rubber stamp things that you have already decided the department will do? Will they contribute to genuine, open discussion to which you will listen with a real desire to be helped in your thinking and planning? Will you be able to prevent them from becoming tediously lengthy opportunities for ritual moaning which does nobody any good – least of all the pupils?

A few moments of thought on this theme reveal pretty quickly that different types of meetings will be required in order to create and maintain an effective department team: the routine meetings, and the 'specials'. The approach to each is different.

Most schools encourage routine weekly or fortnightly departmental or faculty meetings as these establish and support good practice. If you are very lucky, your timetabling colleagues will be able to deliver a non-contact period for all your teachers each week and you can 'claim' that as your meeting slot without any resistance. The reality is that, particularly in a larger department where you may have a blend of full-time and part-time colleagues, you will be unlucky in your search for a timetabled slot, and that one or more senior managers (who are also, incidentally, arguably the ultimate challenge for any HoD!) will *not* be available.

You will then have to work your persuasive charms on the team and earmark a lunchtime or after-school slot for the routine business meetings. In either case, in order to make the most of the time you identify, and to lead a willing crew, you should work to establish a clear set of objectives in the meeting and to lead it purposefully through the set agenda. In this way, all present will feel the value of the meeting and support it with involved attendance.

The 'specials' require more care and forward planning. Whether they are meetings which are necessary to discuss a proposed change of specification for a public examination year group; to review the department development plan and devise the next year's version; to do some 'blue skies' thinking on a specific scheme of work; or even to review the dreaded departmental risk assessment; you will do well to flag up the need for these well in advance – so that those required at each meeting have time to adjust to the notion of the need and to plan their diaries accordingly.

Most colleagues, given ample warning, and being consulted about scheduling, are generally very willing to take part in major meetings of this kind, as long as they can see a useful output, and as long as they feel involved. Indeed, for some topics of discussion, you may feel you can legitimately appoint a smaller sub-group of the department to work without you. Alternatively, you may choose to lead such a group yourself.

Take time to consider if you can make one of these 'specials' into something of a social gathering, too. I know of at least one department in my school that has its annual development planning discussion over a summer holiday luncheon in one or other member's garden, sharing the provision of catering. There are worse ways to spend a day, and the habit is established in the department's calendar, and to great effect.

However, when the need arises for a 'crisis management' meeting, beware of inadvertently trampling on all the goodwill you have generated. Friday at 4pm is *never* a good time for a meeting, even with cream cakes or a stiff gin. Choosing the right location for your formal meetings is important, too. The corner of the staff room, however appealing in terms of proximity to the coffee supplies and biscuits, has the disadvantage of all the distractions of a major school thoroughfare. Be bold and insist on finding a quiet corner. If you have a department office, so much the better. If not, find an empty classroom. There is usually one somewhere, whatever the time-tablers tell you.

Moreover, at the risk of being controversial, the pub is not the forum for a business meeting – although it might well be the place for a bonding discussion after an early evening meeting. That said, be careful that you don't exclude colleagues from such gatherings. Those who have to rush home to look after children/elderly parents/the boarding house they run as 'the night job', or whatever else, can harbour resentments very quickly if they feel they can never be part of a team outing. The answer, once again, is forward planning.

Having established the kind of meeting you wish to hold and having chosen your venue, you then turn to the essential formalities that make your meeting not only a management tool for you, but also a means of communication with senior management – to whom copies of paperwork are likely to be sent, depending on the formal requirements of your school.

The routine meeting will probably require a generic agenda and however overly formal your colleagues think it is, the standard opening items provide a useful record of events: Present (including a note of who was in the chair); Apologies for Absence; Minutes of the last Meeting; Matters Arising.

The item Minutes of the Last Meeting ensures that everyone agrees that minutes are a true account of that event – and thus they cannot later be revisited by those who decide to take you to task over details of semantics or content. The record is set. Matters Arising offers colleagues the chance to report back on any action they have undertaken, as well as to contribute further to any ongoing discussion – and they offer you the chance to signal to team members that they must be prepared to return briefly to earlier items formally to close them off. Identify these clearly on the agenda, but be careful only to take those points which are not already listed as items for the current meeting. If in doubt, put longer items on the main agenda.

Consider having two other set items high up on your agenda to focus the team on the main educational purpose of the department. First, Pupils Causing Concern: this item allows your colleagues to report more formally on those students whom they are most likely to have brought to your attention already via a separate discussion. Equally, others may be brought to the meeting for the first time. Having allowed any grumbling to be aired alongside genuine concerns, focus in quickly on an action plan for each pupil, and ensure it is minuted. Management will very much appreciate your attention to this and may see a pattern emerging for an individual pupil across a number of departments. In addition, your frustrated or discontented colleague will feel supported by the suggestions and affirmation of the whole team. And critically, you will be able to return to these pupils at a future meeting, and your colleagues will then be able to see if the planned action is working, and to what effect.

The second item, Pupils Doing Well, is equally important and is the 'lift' after the list of the concerns. It is always good to remind ourselves of this batch of students – far larger in number than those giving concern – who are making good progress or revealing hidden talents for the subject. Here, any action needed might involve further mentoring or encouragement to be provided by the department. These discussions can ultimately lead on to university applications to read your subject which is always the icing on the departmental cake at the end of any academic year.

Other items will suggest themselves to you, but you may like to ensure that there is at least one item that relates to forward planning or a manageable aspect of the curriculum, in order to focus as much on high-level strategic development as on the more mundane 'housekeeping' tasks.

It is a good idea to seek items for meeting agendas from your colleagues, too. They may have specific points which they wish to discuss more widely, or they may be looking for ideas on a particular scheme of work. As long as these items are added through you, and you have a chance to establish that they will be productive, the shared ownership of the meetings will pay dividends in the longer run to you as the leader, and will enhance the professional morale of your colleagues. You will be seen to be taking them and their ideas seriously.

Finally, consider adding to the foot of your agenda a list of any impending departmental or whole school deadlines as an aide-memoire to your colleagues. In this way you avoid sounding hectoring in the meeting itself. Above all, try to keep the agendas for routine meetings short and manageable.

You can also attach to your agenda any department items which are only a matter of note and which couldn't possibly raise controversial issues, thus saving meeting time for more interesting discussion items. As leader, you are also your colleagues' servant – and you can make life much easier for them by providing regular communication and easy reference guides on any school policy or calendar details in this way.

Where minutes are concerned, different departments have different policies. Where there is a second in department, it may well be his/her role to take minutes. Alternatively, taking turns round the team ensures the burden is spread and the colleague who is embroiled in a major extra-curricular activity that week can be allowed respite until another time. This kind of collaborative approach is usually much appreciated by the whole team.

The style of minutes is a matter of personal preference, and senior management may well issue guidelines. In general though, keep minutes succinct, and ensure that the summary of discussions is concise, with the outcomes/decisions very clearly expressed. Do not shy away, however, from minuting that a range of opinions was expressed on a given topic: otherwise your colleagues may accuse you of a whitewash. Not only that, but senior management will be blissfully unaware that they might need to be involved in an issue at some future stage. Record the requirement for further discussion, or your own need to reflect before making the final decision which you will then expect the group to follow. That is your job, when push comes to shove.

Consider having an action column on the right hand side, with the initials of the person to whom the action falls given in bold so that the minutes form a ready reference document. This also ensures that Matters Arising in the next meeting can be dealt with swiftly, and that those needing to act will be prompted to do so by the need to give an account of their actions at the next meeting. Those who have not yet acted can be gently pursued until they do!

The last thing to consider is how you will manage your meetings. This will be largely determined by your own personal style of leadership, but bear in mind the need to be businesslike and to focus on the agenda. Don't let things wander. All teachers are far too busy to be very tolerant of time-wasting or dithering. If it is 'too difficult', reserve the right to reflect and return. If it is straightforward, don't let anyone hijack that fact with tangential gossip.

At the end of each term, read back over your agendas and minutes of routine meetings, and check that any loose ends of discussions or concerns have been satisfactorily tied up. Spend holiday time, too, planning ahead for any 'special' meetings you may require, including that longer start-of-term slot which is inevitably a blend of both routine and longer items. And ensure that, when you reach your end-of-year meeting to review the development plan, you have kept your colleagues on track with *their* work on that crucial piece of *your* work, so that the meeting can be very much one of proud reflection on things achieved, and excitement about what the future will bring.

If you play your management cards right, it is possible to have a department of contrasting personalities eagerly looking forward to department meetings and working closely together. Remember that much of this is in the careful forward planning as well as the impact of your charming and winsome personality. Good luck!

Chapter 13

Inspection issues in the age of ISI2 and 3

Jill Berry

Leading your departmental team through an Independent Schools Inspectorate (ISI) inspection is one of the most significant challenges that a head of department is likely to face. It is also a tremendous opportunity – to take stock of your effectiveness as a team; for the whole school to receive formal recognition for what you achieve; to analyse where you are at a given point; and to help you focus your energies as you plan for the future.

There is always scope for improvement in what we do and how we do it. Acceptance of this is crucial – as individuals, as departments and within the school as a whole if we are to gain as much as we can from the experience of inspection. We invest a good deal of time, effort, energy and money in this process and we need to learn all we can in order to make such investment fully worthwhile.

The actual form of the inspection has changed, and will continue to change, over time. Under the first cycle, most individual HoDs received verbal feedback from a member of the inspection team, and there was a separate subject report within the (lengthy) full written report. Within the second cycle, introduced in 2007, there are fewer lesson observations and no individual subject feedbacks or separate written reports on subjects.

It is important that HoDs are clear about this, and that you manage the expectations of your departmental members, some of whom may not be observed teaching. If they have experienced a first cycle inspection, they may be expecting the same again and you will need to ensure they are aware of the changes.

At the time of writing, ISI, the Associations and the DCSF are in the process of discussing the shape of the third cycle, and the details are not yet finalised. We do know that independent school inspections will need to be more frequent (possibly every three years) with a much shorter notice period (days or weeks rather than months). However, whatever the actual form of the inspection that emerges, the basic principles are unlikely to change.

Even with fewer lesson observations and no individual subject feedback or written reports, observation of the teaching within the school is a vital part of the inspection week as the team inspectors, under the guidance of the reporting inspector, assess the extent to which the school delivers what it claims to do. The inspectors will look at the school's stated aims and objectives and, during the course of an intense period of inspection, they will come to conclusions about how well the school meets these aims. They will observe lessons. They will analyse a considerable amount of pupil work and how it is assessed (looking closely both at work in individual subjects and also looking across curriculum areas to evaluate the provision across a section of the school).

The work of the department in contributing to the overall educational experience of an inspection is still important. Inspectors will also want to know how priorities in the school development plan are being pursued within each department. They will look at documentation, and they will hold interviews with pupils and staff. Although the final written report (considerably shorter under ISI2, and so more easily digestible) will not include sections on individual departments, it will, nevertheless, include examples from lessons to illustrate its judgements.

The report will comment on the quality of teaching and assessment, pupils' learning and achievements and the pupils' spiritual, moral, social and cultural education in order to draw its conclusions about the educational experience the school provides. The inspectors will also look at the quality of leadership and management within the school, so your personal contribution as HoD will be relevant to this, too.

We all appreciate that an inspection report is a snapshot in time. Schools obviously hope that it will be an accurate snapshot, which is also as positive as possible. Of course we polish up our shoes for an inspection, but what we need to present is 'our best face, not a false face'. The inspectors will also be keen to assess the extent to which we are honestly aware of both our strengths and the areas in which we still need most to develop.

School self-evaluation is increasingly important in both the maintained and independent sectors. Inspection may focus our minds, but the questions it encourages us to ask ourselves are questions we should be asking anyway. We want to do a good job for the sake of the pupils we teach. At inspection time we clearly want to be *seen* to do a good job. We also want to be constantly looking for ways in which we can do an even better job. Inspection can help us to do this, so being honest with the inspection team, and with ourselves, is crucial.

As a useful starting point, try asking yourselves the following questions:

• Within the department, what do we already do well? (Focus, perhaps, on three areas at the most).

• How do we know?

• What could we do better? (Again, focus on no more than three areas).

• How do we know?

• Where would we like to be in 12 months'/two years'/three years' time?

• How will we know when we've got there?

Perhaps answer these questions yourself first, and then discuss them as a department. It may be interesting to see how much consensus there is. Ensure you involve fully any support staff who work with your department; they are clearly important members of your team and they will be contributing to the inspection and will need support and reassurance too. If you're in a four to 18 or seven to 18 school, liaise with your subject co-ordinator, if there is one, in the junior school section.

This kind of self-evaluation discussion will certainly help you to consider, as a group, your priorities and perceptions. It may also give you a clearer idea about where you're heading and what you hope, as a department, to get out of the experience of inspection.

An inspection is an opportunity to take stock and it is useful in advance of the inspection to think about your departmental documentation. Are you content that it is up-to-date, an accurate reflection of how you operate and a helpful guide to current staff, to new staff entering the department, or perhaps to a trainee teacher on a temporary placement within the department?

Producing glossy material to impress the inspection team is not a good use of your time, but ensuring that your departmental handbook and schemes of work serve their purpose as working documents certainly is. Think about your administrative systems, for example the minuting of departmental meetings and whether you use the minutes to ensure items which are debated are helpfully followed up.

Departmental monitoring and observation is potentially a sensitive area, but it is difficult to dispute that an effective HoD should have a secure grasp of what is going on in the classrooms of all members of their team. If you are asked about the strengths and weaknesses of departmental teaching, can you give clear and confident responses which are supported by evidence – again, come back to the question 'How do you know?' What support do you give those who need it? How are you helping the individual members of your team to be the best they can and to develop their skills?

These may be members of staff who have been teaching longer than you have. We cannot assume that those who need most guidance are those with the least teaching experience. How do you make the most of the strengths within your team, too? Crucially, what are you doing to ensure that the pupils in your classrooms are getting the best deal they can? This should lead to a useful debate about what we understand to be high quality teaching and learning in our subject. Do remember, too, that every one of us may teach an inadequate lesson occasionally, and that we all need a degree of humility about this.

The inspectors will observe lessons and consider how effective the department is as they arrive at their overall judgements about the school. Your awareness of the effectiveness of the team is also relevant to your success as its leader.

In some subject areas there may be a good deal of team teaching and a philosophy of open doors whereby you, and other staff, frequently visit each other's lessons. In other subject areas, or other schools, there may be a very different culture and some defensiveness about the invasion of our 'territory'.

As a new Head I carried out a pupil pursuit exercise whereby I shadowed one pupil in each year group for a day. This was a helpful way of getting into classrooms and focusing on the pupils' experience rather than primarily the teachers' performance. It is also worth remembering that we can observe each other in order to pick up good ideas ourselves, rather than the focus always being judgement of and feedback to the teacher observed. Watching others teach always encourages us to reflect on our own practice.

You might consider some paired observation across the department (including you, of course), whereby colleagues watch each other teach and evaluate the experience. In this context it is worth using the same type of lesson observation forms which the team inspectors themselves will be using. You can access them from the ISI website (www.isi.org.uk). They will also help you to consider the questions the inspectors will be asking themselves within the classroom.

This should generate some useful discussion within the department and should also help to prepare your staff for the lesson observations which will take place within the inspection. Remember, though (as I mentioned earlier), that some teachers may not be observed, and they will need your support, too. At the start of the inspection teachers find this last point difficult to believe, but it is those who are not seen until later in the week, or who are not seen at all, who are usually the most twitchy, and those who are not observed can feel a great sense of anti-climax rather than a sense of their good fortune at having 'escaped'.

The inspectors will be looking at a cross-section of work to evaluate how effective assessment is, in addition to how varied, well-planned and stimulating the written tasks are. Consider how comfortable you feel with your awareness of how successfully the different members of the department apply the established assessment policies and criteria. We are all now used to cross-moderation at GCSE and A level, as appropriate, which is helpful, but some cross-moderation of work by younger pupils is also a useful way into a discussion about the effectiveness of our feedback, perhaps within the context of how well we are using *Assessment for Learning,* if appropriate.

What does our marking say about us? The inspectors will certainly be evaluating this when they scrutinise the sample of work (across different age groups and across the ability range) and when they talk to the pupils themselves. Think about how, as a department, you can prepare for this and take the temperature yourselves before the inspection team arrives. Could your marking and assessment practices be more effective – for the sake of your learners and not just because of the inspectors?

We should not, of course, try to prepare the pupils for their meetings with the inspectors, or grill them afterwards! But listening to the pupils is always a very useful starting point when we are taking stock of how we work and how successfully we are meeting the learners' needs. In terms of our self-evaluation and our developing awareness of our strengths and areas for development, receptiveness to what our pupils think in advance of the inspection is a very positive strategy.

It may be that we want to consult them about a particular course, about assessment methods, about how they learn best. Focused discussion (perhaps in small groups followed by careful feedback), appropriate questionnaires which are analysed and the findings debated, and a general openness to, rather than defensiveness in the face of, pupil opinion will help us to check on what we do and show others that we are committed to securing improvement. In addition, if pupils are accustomed to being consulted they are likely to cope more equably with the questions from the inspectors!

So far, the issues considered and action suggested have all been concerned with what you might do in advance of the inspection: thinking about self-evaluation; checking your documentation; considering your monitoring and awareness of the effectiveness of your departmental team both within the classroom and in terms of the work set and assessed; listening to the pupils. Now assume that you have done all this and that you feel as confident and well-prepared as possible when the week arrives. What can you do during the week itself to ensure that the inspection experience is as positive as it can be for you and your departmental team?

First, be positive yourself and enjoy the opportunity it will give you to enthuse in the classroom, perhaps to talk about your role, your priorities and convictions. Set the tone within the department and be open and receptive to the experience. Support your departmental team, encouraging its members to talk about how observed lessons or conversations with inspectors have gone. Again, don't forget staff whose responsibilities are other than teaching. Support those who have not yet been seen so they do not feel left out.

Support your senior leadership team by sharing experiences with them and keeping them in the loop too: the Head, for example, can feel a little adrift during the week itself when it is all finally happening. One of my warming memories from our last inspection week was our examinations officer, a robust Lancastrian woman, passing me in the corridor and saying: "Is it all going well, or would you like a hug?" (Remember, though, that offering your Head a hug will depend on the nature of your relationship...)

In terms of how your department fares, once the week is under way this is probably outside your control. I remember as a Head feeling as if a huge liner had pulled away from the dock, and that all I could do was wave my hankie and hope it didn't turn out to be the *Titanic*. So do your teaching, answer the inspectors' questions, be positive and keep smiling.

Your Head, members of the governing body and senior leadership team will attend an oral feedback session at the end of the week and will be able to report back some headline judgements. Take the opportunity to show your appreciation for the work of your team and the contribution of the pupils.

The Head will subsequently receive a draft of the written report, within which (s)he will be able to correct any factual inaccuracies, but they will not be able to question any judgements. In due course this will be published on the ISI website and made available to all interested parties and your Head will no doubt comment on it, both publicly and internally.

When you read the written report you need to consider how your department has contributed to the final judgements and what contribution you can make to the carrying out of the *next steps* and any recommendations. You need to see the report as a jumping off point for future development – how can the school, and your department, move forward in the light of the inspectors' findings?

Occasionally you may feel a judgement is over-harsh, but I do believe you can take steps to address such criticism in ways which will still take you forward. I remember being very impressed by a Head's response to an inspection report which commented on a negative parental perception of some element of the school's provision. The inspectors found no evidence that the provision was wanting, but the Head determined that if the parental perception was that this was not all it should be, the school had to take action to address the misperception. This is the kind of receptiveness to criticism to which I think we should aspire.

Remember that the process is even more important than the end product of the written report. Consider, and perhaps discuss with the department, what you feel you have gained from the entire process, including the self-evaluation and internal monitoring elements in addition to the experience of observation and consultation during the week itself. The central issue, in terms of the quality of teaching and learning, is how can we make sure satisfactory lessons move towards being good ones, good to very good, very good to excellent. This is a drive in which we should all be engaged, and the inspection should help us.

If in the future, as seems inevitable, we have far shorter notice of when an inspection will take place (though if inspections are three-yearly we will be able to take a good guess as to which term our next inspection will fall in), our preparation for inspection will be something which is on-going rather than carried out once notice of an inspection date is received. Again, this is no bad thing – all the suggestions above about evaluation of our own progress are good practice and should help us to ensure that we are working as effectively as possible, something which is in everyone's best interests.

Finally, if in the future you have had three years' or more experience of whole school issues and senior management, consider training as a team inspector with ISI yourself. It is a tremendous experience, a real privilege to have the opportunity to visit other schools and sit in their classrooms and talk to their staff and pupils. It will help you to contribute to the success of others, and to reflect on what happens in your own school and to bring good ideas back. This element of peer review is a vital part of what makes ISI inspections special, and, although the future is still open to debate, there appears to be a great deal of support for peer review across the different Associations and within ISI itself.

So see inspection as an opportunity rather than an inconvenience, and be open to what you can gain from it, both within the department, across your schools and as individuals. I wish you well in your inspection experiences.

Chapter 14

Two perspectives from bursars:

What bursars do

Margot Chaundler

'Bad money drives out good.'
Gresham's law, after Sir Thomas Gresham 1519-1579.

To begin with: a set of assumptions. First, that bursars and heads of department have one thing in common: their roles and importance in a school have grown dramatically in recent years. Secondly, that as budget responsibilities have increasingly been devolved to HoDs, it has become more important that bursars and HoDs have mutual respect and a good working relationship. And thirdly, that an atmosphere of fruitful co-operation and a sense of common purpose are most likely to exist where the HoD knows the overall context in which a bursar has to operate.

The appellation 'bursar' derives from the Latin *bursa*, meaning purse. According to the *Pocket Oxford Dictionary*, it is the title of the treasurer of a college. However, the role of a modern bursar is a good deal wider, covering not just financial management but human resource management; management of the school buildings and estate; and the delivery of the whole infrastructure of what is, nowadays, a multi-million pound business of increasing dimension and complexity. The maintenance of the IT network across the school site could also form part of his responsibilities.

The bursar is likely to have responsibility for a team of perhaps some 60 or so assorted professional and blue-collar staff, more in larger schools. Some will work very part-time, others will be full-time, and they range widely from graduate professionals, such as accountants and engineers, to grounds and cleaning staff. All require managing and motivating – a task that can become incredibly time-consuming.

Practically all bursars are on their second careers, and they have usually been selected for their record of financial and management experience. They may well have occupied responsible roles which have given them considerable exposure to high-level strategic and forward planning, where they have acquired a range of skills that are transferable to the education sector.

According to the ISBA's web publication *How to Become a Bursar*: 'About 40% of bursars are ex-armed forces, with the next largest grouping being chartered accountants. Other bursars come from a very wide variety of backgrounds including banking, financial services, manufacturing, hotel management, engineers and surveyors.' Many are motivated by strong feelings of altruism and a desire 'to give something back' during the last phase of their working lives.

The bursar is appointed by the school's governors, and remains accountable to them for the financial management of the school and for the delivery of the school's infrastructure. He, or increasingly she, usually works through the Head to the chairman of governors (or chairman of the finance committee), although in some schools the bursar reports only to the governors. However, irrespective of the model, the bursar indisputably occupies the third position in the complex triangular relationship involving the chairman of governors and the Head, and the wise bursar is careful to respect this.

That said, the right of direct access to the chairman of governors means that the bursar occupies a unique position within a school's hierarchy. The bursar will probably speak to, or have email contact with, the chairman of governors on a weekly basis. No one else in the school community, apart from the Head, occupies such a position, and the onus is very much on the bursar to ensure that the Head, especially a new Head, finds this unique role both helpful and supportive, as opposed to the opposite.

The bursar usually acts as clerk to the governors and as secretary to the various governors' sub-committees and trusts. (S)he is responsible for ensuring that the governors and the school remain at all times compliant with the financial, employment, health and safety and planning regulations. This is an increasing burden, when the bursar is faced with a seemingly unending torrent of new regulations emanating from both the British and European parliaments.

There may be issues relating to the governance of the school, for example, with non-teaching staff pensions, on which the bursar deals exclusively with the chairman of governors. Generally though, the bursar should be careful to involve the Head, or at least to ensure that (s)he knows in advance what is happening. Few of us like to be taken by surprise, and parallel and sideways communication is an important part of a bursar's role. Thankfully, the ubiquitous email makes this task a great deal simpler.

The bursar's multi-faceted role, his previous experience and above all, his role of preparing agendas and papers for governors' meetings, means that he is well placed to contribute to discussion on the strategic direction and forward planning of the school. He knows the individual governors far better than any of the other school staff, apart from the Head. In addition, his daily working contacts with the school's professional advisers, such as lawyers, accountants, architects, surveyors and not least, its bankers, shape his thinking rather differently from the influences that inform his colleagues on the senior management team, most, if not all of whom, have spent a lifetime in the education sector.

A major strength of the independent sector is its long-serving and devoted staff. Indeed, it is quite common to encounter teachers who have spent 20 or more years in one school, and who have never taught in the maintained sector. It is not surprising that they have not developed the skills of managing budgets or managing staff; the bursar himself may possess an academic degree from a good university but needs to remind himself regularly that he has chosen a different career path entirely, of his own volition, if mutual incomprehension is to be avoided.

'But it is pretty to see what money will do.'
Samuel Pepys' Diary, 21st March 1667.

The Head is responsible for filling the school, and his or her success in this function is critical to the school's survival. Unfortunately, not all schools do survive, usually due to a combination of factors, some of which, such as location, are not of the Head's making. However, unsound financial strategy, or over-ambitious plans for development, can often lie at the root of the difficulties. Being a charity does not render an independent school immune from the normal pressures of the market place and, ultimately, the bursar may have to face up to the challenge of pointing out the unpleasant truth that it is against the law to trade whilst bankrupt.

A sound financial strategy has therefore to be the highest strategic priority of any school. All school development plans need a strong reality check. This is an area where the diplomatic skills of the bursar can be tested to their limits as (s)he attempts to steer a difficult course between loyally supporting an ambitious Head, and urging the need for financial caution.

An independent school needs to make an operating surplus if it is to survive, and it can only pay its staff – which typically accounts for at least 70% of expenditure in a day school – if it can recruit sufficient numbers of fee-paying pupils to generate that surplus. The single most important strategic decision that a school's governors have to make each year is to set the fee rise and the staff pay rise, and to look at cash projections for the next five to ten years that include both, and perhaps a number of modelled alternatives.

Governors need to see sensitivity analyses that model the impact of the fee rise and pupil numbers on the bottom line. Producing this data is the responsibility of the bursar and his finance team. It is also important that the school's SMT understands that it takes, for example, three additional pupils' fees to pay for one extra youngish member of the teaching staff.

They also need to understand that such is the effect of what is known as 'incremental drift' that it will eventually take four and finally, five, pupils to pay for that teacher as he or she progresses up the pay spine. Many teachers do not appreciate that incremental pay is nowadays comparatively rare outside the public sector. The fact that exactly the same post can be filled by a qualified teacher earning twice as much as another equally well-qualified teacher has the potential to distort a school's budget significantly.

The surplus or cash that is available after the operating expenses have been met is needed to fund the maintenance and upgrading of the school, capital programmes for its expansion and development, and perhaps to endow bursaries, or a sinking fund for future building work. The bursar has a major role in formulating these programmes, working closely to take account of the aspirations and plans of the Head and the SMT. He will also have his own list of defects that need rectifying, such as roof replacement, asbestos removal and cyclical maintenance.

Close cooperation and good communications are essential in this area as priorities are established and compromises made. Heads of department are involved in discussions about plans that affect them; but the Head or the director of studies is likely to remain closely involved in the detail. It is also observable, to an extent that might surprise the new bursar, how much influence some of the members of individual academic departments can have in this process.

The bursar has an important role in making HoDs understand that programmes cannot be altered after the contract has been let, without considerable penalty in money and time; as well as conveying the truism that the quiet power tool has not yet been invented!

The annual departmental budgeting round is a useful opportunity to educate HoDs in financial reality. It generally occurs in the late autumn, and may or may not involve the bursar personally. Where the director of studies is the overall budget holder for academic budgets, this task may be undertaken by him, dealing with his subordinate budget holders, and perhaps assisted by the school's accountant.

This is because the overall director of studies' budget is probably no more than 12% of the overall school's expenditure, and even the budgets of the largest academic department are quite modest and uncomplicated, compared with the school's capital plans, expenditure on maintenance and investment in IT. The school could well spend more than twice as much on catering as it spends on its academic budgets. It follows therefore that involving the bursar in the annual round of academic budgeting may not be the most productive use of his time, particularly as the average director of studies will have a pretty good idea of how he wishes to carve up his pot to his subordinate budget holders.

It is worth adding in parenthesis that academic budgets are comparatively small because they do not cover staff costs, the costs of IT, photocopying or pupils' text books. Setting up individual departmental cost centres which show that it costs more to teach PE or science, than, say, classics, is unlikely to lead to more effective financial management, and will certainly not improve the quality of teaching. It will, however, consume a great deal of senior management time. By contrast, effective monitoring of expenditure, and ensuring that budget holders stick to their budgets, or agree variances in advance, is essential.

"A bank is a place that will lend you money if you can prove that you don't need it."
Bob Hope.

The governors will expect the bursar to spend the majority of his time dealing with both financial and non-financial implications of major maintenance programmes and, above all, in capital programmes and in organising and running the school's infrastructure. Arranging capital programmes is a lengthy process, involving a team of professional advisers, as well as bankers if funding is required. A school may have a proud history, a full role and all the elements for success, but banks require a great deal of detail from a school's lawyers and accountants before lending money. Providing all of this can be time-consuming for the bursar, particularly if a 'beauty parade' of several competing banks is involved.

"Events, dear boy. Events."
Harold Macmillan, Prime Minister 1957-63, on being asked to what his biggest problem was attributed.

This chapter has touched upon some of the strategic and planning aspects of the bursar's role. Inevitably though, it is the mass of daily trivia that crowds the bursar's life: the chasing parents for fees; assessing parental entitlement to financial support; human resources; property maintenance and the continuous succession of staff management crises, usually involving cleaning and catering staff, some of which could be the subject of a separate and perhaps more light-hearted chapter. But the author of this chapter felt that a record in random events had been reached with the following email from her catering manager:

> *'Dear Bursar,*
> *I have in my office the remains of Colin Peter McEvedy who was left on the window sill in the dining room. Do you know who he belongs to, or what I should do with the ashes?'*

All in a bursar's day's work...

How to keep your bursar happy

Shane Rutter-Jerome

The Bursar says "no" in one of 55 different ways; but (s)he probably won't feel so inclined to do so if you prepare the ground by talking about your department and explaining your cunning plan. From the bursar's end it all looks so different, and perhaps seeing it from that perspective as well as your own might make running a department easier.

Whilst heads of department might dream of an unlimited budget, the reality is that the school is likely to be able to afford only to allocate the minimum resources thought necessary to achieve the result required: result being defined appropriately. But thought by *whom* to be necessary? Certainly not the bursar, who will not wish to be drawn into the mire of inter-departmental rivalry. Here be dragons, which the bursar may not wish to slay.

Broadly speaking, planning in the school takes place on two levels: the school strategic plan (possibly with a three- to five-year development plan updated annually) provides the way ahead and then the annual budget is the practical outcome. You have a part to play in both.

In most schools, the annual budgetary process will involve some rigorous haggling, overseen by the director of studies. If conducted thoroughly, this will involve departmental funding – probably the least costly of the actual resources (well below staff costs and provision and maintenance of teaching space) but the one most easily measured – being calculated on the basis of pupil numbers, activity levels and syllabus demands.

From time to time, or perhaps even annually, the governing body may decree that a process of 'zero budgeting' is to be applied. In practice, this might take one of two quite different forms. The least taxing involves a zero increase over the previous year's financial allocation, except where a clearly identified new requirement exists. More testing is the version in which all departments have to justify why they need any funding at all: start with zero and justify what you need.

This may sound ridiculous but experienced staff will be well aware of some departmental budgets which have grown annually without any real control and which have become over-funded in relation to other departments. Given a fair and logical director of studies, neither zero budgets nor the normal annual process need cause any great concern to a HoD who has thought through the coming year (and the next, if change is coming).

A head of department has responsibility for a range of resources and has differing levels of influence over these and over their application. The actual budget may be tiny in cash terms. Crucial to making progress are addressing the requirement and understanding the system. Much of this publication is rightly concerned with managing staff and curriculum issues. These are important areas of both planning and day-to-day leadership and management.

If you have technicians, secretarial staff or classroom assistants, they may come under the bursar's management, so keep contact if there are any concerns. With major issues, such as teaching and managing staff and pupils, it is easy to forget the other aspects of planning ahead for the department and of running it on a daily basis.

Once in post, you will have thought about your department, perhaps putting your thoughts into a proper departmental plan. This will involve staff and training, physical teaching resources, and a mix of longer term aims and short term targets. It may have to fit in with a larger faculty plan and it will certainly have to dovetail in with the overall school plan. Crucially, it will allow you, and senior management, to see clearly your priorities and where you are going. How much you can achieve will depend on how costly it is and on how well you put your case for resources.

As you develop the plan, both short term and long, and as you seek to gain clearance for it, you will need to understand 'the system'. This includes the procedures for funding and planning development; for funding equipment; for allocation of your annual budget; and for authorising and monitoring spending. Understanding the system also implies learning who allocates resources – and how – and thus how to approach and convince the decision makers.

Ask for a copy of the school's financial instruction (and then follow it). The key words here are forward (and) planning: if you look ahead and think your ideas through, you have at least a chance of achieving aims which match those of the school. It will be important that others share your vision. If you are instigating change, then some may be less enthusiastic than others; you will have to think through how to persuade the dissenters or how to overcome or bypass their concerns. Or you will have to modify your plan until it becomes more widely acceptable.

In this, an understanding of your departmental staff views, the views and priorities of the Head and senior management and the thrust of the school development plan or strategic plan will remind you that your plan is but one cog in a larger machine. If you arrive in the middle of a large scale development of the school, it may be some time before your plans materialise; in which case you might relax and work harder on the short-term aspects, as there may be some sympathy with your wishes but no money to fund them – yet.

This leads us rather deviously back to the first part of this contribution: achieving an appropriate share of the budget. There is no substitute for early discussion with the director of studies, the Head, the bursar, and anyone else who can help you achieve your well-thought-out plan. Whilst it is true that bursars have to say "no" rather more often than they might like, this is largely because, once the budget is set, they have little scope for redirecting money.

Governors sign up to a budget based on pupil numbers and then make an allocation of funds to support it. Any change has to be justified and, if there is not a compensating reduction elsewhere, it is difficult to fund anything not thought about in the budget process. Heads of creative departments beware: you may be prone to sudden inspiration; this is exciting, but is no substitute for proper planning.

Bursars are not hugely fond of surprises (although a bottle of something nice on a 'big' birthday rarely misses the target). Financial planning means just what it says. But like senior civil servants, bursars enjoy the (almost) intellectual challenge of helping those who want to be helped. They may feel a warm glow if asked for advice on how to bid for resources, on lead times, and on other sources of funding, providing that it is clear that you are not just trying to bypass the Head and director of studies.

Bursars will be pleased if you can back up your ideas with research on cost and effectiveness. They will feel that some progress is being made if you monitor and control your department's spending and, like most staff, they and their support staff chiefs will welcome a word of thanks at appropriate moments.

Finally, a few dos and don'ts:

- Do speak to the bursar and finance staff regularly.
- Do look carefully at plans for development affecting your department *early* in the process; time spent at this stage saves angst and money.
- Do follow the system and controls laid down in the financial instructions.
- Do research the cost and sources of equipment authorised in the budget.
- Do master the system for minor works and repairs; report faults promptly and explain why you need work done.
- Do identify the department's needs at or before the end of term, not when you come back to work.
- Do look after any support staff working in your department.
- Do give early warning of any additional support needed for events mounted by your department: no surprises!
- Do remember that, like you, the support staff like to be thanked occasionally.
- Do allow your enthusiasm to show; it can light up all around you.
- Don't be downcast if your cunning plan does not pass muster first time; it might just be the wrong timing in the bigger school scheme.

And, if you manage your budget, and learn how the system works, with luck, you may be allocated funds next year, too!

Afterword

Brenda Despontin

The first two volumes of this series on *Leading Schools in the 21st Century* explored the changing roles and responsibilities of those who shape educational provision at the most senior level in independent schools today. But the real change in educational leadership nationally in the last few decades has been at middle management level.

Leadership that is distributed throughout a school requires heads of department and other middle managers to plan strategically; set targets; develop colleagues; budget effectively; and contribute to whole-school management matters. It is a far cry now from the days when my first departmental head regularly locked himself away at lunchtime in his 'office' (an airless stock cupboard) comforted by his pipe and the day's cricket commentary on the department's only radio. Having completed his annual duty of ordering a few text books (usually tried and tested – nothing too modern), and after teaching the Oxbridge hopefuls, he left the rest of us to fend for ourselves. 'Futures thinking' was not high on his agenda.

In this volume, Michael Carslaw has examined the 21st-century middle manager's duty to review staff performance, set targets and monitor. Paul Todd described the importance of leading by example and Melanie Lincoln reflected on her middle management experience. All these in their separate ways highlight the difference between being a passionate subject specialist, dedicated to the delivery of a section of the school's curriculum and determined to make a difference in young lives, and that new, overall responsibility for the subject's place in the curriculum, together with its delivery by *others* who may be neither as passionate nor as competent. The change from classroom manager of pupils to middle manager of people is not to be underestimated.

'People skills' are essential for effective departmental leadership, not just subject expertise as of yore. Edward Elliott explored the importance of supporting young staff members in the department, where mentoring towards QTS or for the GTP requires time, an awareness of recent educational theory and practice, and the art of delivering constructive criticism that will sound like positive encouragement.

Equally important are the competencies to handle meetings effectively, as outlined by Alice Phillips. Nothing irritates teachers more than meetings which are time-wasting and are managed poorly, and there are some simple ways, included in this chapter, by which such pitfalls can be avoided. It pays to know where the fast balls might be stored, to prepare well, and keep to the agenda.

Then there are the staff who are underachieving or generally 'coasting' and who need steering back onto track. Some of those may have been colleagues and friends before an internal promotion for the head of department. Some may be older and more experienced, or may have been internal candidates if the appointment went to an outsider.

Some may be coping with personal difficulties outside the school walls. All are complex, and challenging, but poor performance is ignored at a head of department's peril: it does not just go away. Be sympathetic where appropriate, but be professional, and follow agreed procedures to the letter. It never fails to keep firmly in mind at all times the question: what best meets the needs of the pupils here?

Jane Gandee wrote of the importance of schemes of work, the composition of which can be shared by all members of the department, and reviewed regularly via standing items in departmental meetings to ensure everyone is on board. Similarly, a number of contributors touched on the importance of continuous professional development with regular individual staff reviews, which include lesson observations. A departmental policy of regular peer assessment (which involves more than just the HoD observing colleagues) is good practice, but it is successful only when non-threatening and when it leads to open exchange of ideas, resources and expertise.

Communication is a constant challenge in all schools, made easier perhaps by modern technology. But there is always the dilemma of 'Who needs to know this?' which pastoral managers in particular ask on a daily basis. In a big faculty such as that described by Nick Fisher, or with a diverse pastoral team, perhaps on a split site, the challenge can be daunting, and special care is needed to include part-time staff, or support staff where any decision impacts on their role.

Kathryn Macaulay emphasised the growing importance of ICT in managing people at all levels. But it is a huge cost centre for a school; a financial equivalent of a black hole. Heads of department need to keep up with recent trends and developments, to be trained adequately themselves and to enthuse openly about the ICT benefits in their subject. But they need to facilitate training opportunities for others too, including any support staff attached to that subject area.

All such matters cost money, and it quickly becomes apparent to any new head of department that managing the budget will be a high priority. The relationship with the bursar has become increasingly more important, especially where bids for ICT provision are concerned, or where departmental risk assessments need to be completed, or where major departmental refurbishment is under consideration. Both Margot Chaundler and Shane Rutter-Jerome wrote of the role of the bursar in the life of a middle manager today.

Andrew Grant reminded HoDs that however passionate they might be to introduce the latest examination package, or a new subject to sixth form curriculum, such zeal necessitates an awareness of the impact this change will have on the whole school through option choices and staffing. A really effective middle manager sees the bigger picture, even though he continues to fight his corner where necessary.

Leading from the middle is a busy role, because heads of department often have significant teaching responsibilities too. Keeping fresh and up to date will bring rewards, and encouraging debate by occasionally presenting a paper at a head of department meeting, for example, prevents complacency and the dreaded slow decline into pedagogical apathy.

Frances Green wrote from the perspective of a librarian also given responsibility for the gifted and talented programme. She is part of a staff study skills group exploring such concepts as learning styles, gender differences in learning, and multiple intelligences. The chance to report at head of department meetings on these topical issues engenders healthy debate even amongst the cynics.

Sooner or later, the middle manager faces inspection, explored in Jill Berry's chapter, and in truth the visit should not involve much extra work if the department already operates a culture of evaluation and self-assessment, with regularly refreshed schemes of work, good data analysis in place, and proactive professional development in evidence. It should provide an opportunity to showcase the successes of the teaching and learning at work, and to receive justifiable external recognition for a job done well.

Middle managers are the backbone of the school; the solid link between senior leaders and the staffroom. Their growing responsibilities are challenging and manifold, but the job satisfaction is huge. It might be felt when a new initiative, proposed at a curriculum working party, is adopted by all, or when a new teacher leaves after a few years' guidance to be a head of department himself. It might occur when a colleague, formerly a Luddite who needed lots of gentle 'buddying' in ICT, morphs into an enthusiast demanding all departmental correspondence becomes electronic.

Finally, though many will wish to remain at middle manager level, and enjoy all that it holds, others will be confident enough with their growing management and leadership skills to move on. Earlier volumes may then hold some advice and guidance on how best to approach the next step. Without doubt, the challenges of managing a department or a pastoral team in independent schools today provide a solid base for career progress, and offer invaluable, infinitely better training than was to be had in those days of lunchtime cricket commentaries in the stock cupboard.

NOTES

NOTES